W9-CAF-995

Better Homes and Gardens®

A Cross-Stitch CHRISTMAS®

Needlework Treasures

Elizabeth M. Bird 2003

Better Homes and Gardens® Creative Collection™
Des Moines, Iowa

Better Homes and Gardens®

A Cross-Stitch CHRISTMAS®

Our Mark of Excellence seal assures you that every project in this book has been constructed and checked under the direction of the cross-stitch experts at *Better Homes and Gardens® Creative Collection™*.

For book editorial questions, write
Better Homes and Gardens® A Cross-Stitch Christmas® 2003
1716 Locust Street – GA 200, Des Moines, IA 50309-3023;
phone 800/688-6611, Option 2; fax 515/284-3045.
For additional copies or billing questions, call 800/322-0691

First Edition Printing Number and Year: 5 4 3 2 1 04 03 02 01
ISSN:1081-468X
ISBN: 0-696-21619-1

A Cross-Stitch Christmas®

Contents

Page 10 Page 32 Page 59

Christmas *is a magical time,*

rich with rituals and treasured family traditions. There's no other time like it, with its warm wishes, gifts of love, and enchanting decorations. Whatever Christmas means to you, at its heart are peace and love.

If you like to create a personal Christmas each year by stitching beautiful gifts and decorations, you know that Christmas can be a hectic climax of celebration and gift giving. There's plenty of time to plan and begin stitching your Christmas projects now, so you can relax and share wholeheartedly in the joy and celebration. The secret is getting a head start—and keeping organized along the way. Knowing that you have plenty of time before the holiday, you can make exquisite gifts and accessories—each of heirloom quality and a personal expression of appreciation and love.

To help you create your own festive trims and treasured keepsakes, we've assembled a collection of fabulous ornaments and decorations to suit every taste and skill level. We worked with many talented designers to bring you the most beautiful and charming projects you'll see this year. You'll find decorating and gift ideas for young and old, and everyone in between. We're pleased that you've included us in your holiday preparations. Read on to discover how you can begin crafting your own

Needlework Treasures.

Page 76

Page 99

Whatever your holiday decorating style, you're certain to find a favorite in this festive collection of Christmas cross-stitch projects.

Symbols of the season

One joyous message of the holiday season is the warm togetherness of a loving family. The first Christmas family with their humble beginnings is the essence of that spirit of love. Close your eyes for a minute and think of Christmas. What images come to mind? For all of us, the familiar symbols evoke cherished memories of time spent with loved ones. We hope the designs in this chapter will rekindle happy holiday memories and perhaps inspire new ones.

Project instructions begin on page 14.

Design: Donna Vermillion Giampa, Vermillion Stitchery • Photography: Hopkins Associates

Running short on time?
Why not stitch a portion of the
stocking chart as time allows.
Then frame the piece as
shown on the cover.

Symbols of the season

A little bit of whimsy and a whole lot of charm characterize this spectacular stocking *left.* This nostalgic Santa is for many of us the image of Christmas as seen through a child's eyes. The subtle shading makes him so real you'll almost expect to see him wink. Finished with a generous cuff of quilted red fabric and red piping, it's certain to become a well-loved part of your family traditions for years to come. The coordinating ornaments *right* are treasures themselves, and would make thoughtful gifts.

Project instructions begin on page 16.

Design: Carol Emmer • Photography: Hopkins Associates

hope peace happiness love

The delicate pastel hues of this adorable snow angel are far from the traditional reds and greens of the season. But her message of Hope-Peace-Happiness-Love is a universal one. Stitch the piece as shown *opposite* and frame it. Or stitch just the angel to create the sweet ornament *above*.

Project instructions begin on page 18.

Design: Gail Bussi • Photography: opposite, *Dean Tanner;* above, *Hopkins Associates*

Dress up a purchased place mat and napkin in style with motifs from the Patchwork Cardinal Tray as shown *above.* A single snowflake motif stitched over one thread of fabric turns leftover bits of fabric and paper into eye-catching place cards or gift tags.

Project instructions begin on page 19.
Design: Laura Holtorf Collins • Photography: Hopkins Associates

Give your kitchen a folk-art holiday look. We've finished this charming patchwork design as a tray, *opposite,* but you could easily turn it into a wall hanging or pillow as well. Or use the motifs to adorn towels, hot pads, and containers.

Project instructions begin on page 24
Design: Laura Holtorf Collins • Photography: Hopkins Associates

Symbols of the season

Nativity

Materials

16×18" piece of 28-count navy Jobelan fabric
Cotton embroidery floss
DMC spooled metallic thread
Desired frame

Instructions

Center and stitch the Nativity chart *opposite* on the fabric. Use two plies of floss to work the stitches over two threads of the fabric unless otherwise specified. Press the stitched piece from the back. Frame the piece as desired.

Nativity Key

ANCHOR	DMC
CROSS-STITCH (2X)	
002	000 White
342	211 Lavender
1049	301 Medium mahogany
218	319 Dark pistachio
215	320 True pistachio
013	321 True Christmas red
217	367 Medium pistachio
214	368 Light pistachio
1043	369 Pale pistachio
351	400 Dark mahogany
1047	402 Light mahogany
374	420 Medium hazel
372	422 Light hazel
370	434 Medium caramel
1046	435 True caramel
1045	436 Light caramel
362	437 Pale caramel
047	498 Dark Christmas red
098	554 Violet
1064	597 Medium turquoise
1062	598 Light turquoise
393	640 Medium beige-gray
392	642 True beige-gray
391	644 Light beige-gray
046	666 Red
298	725 Medium topaz
295	726 True topaz
293	727 Light topaz
361	738 Tan
1012	754 Medium peach
336	758 Terra-cotta
1021	761 Salmon
309	781 Dark Christmas gold
307	783 True Christmas gold
358	801 True coffee brown
045	814 Dark garnet
390	822 Pale beige-gray
906	869 Dark hazel
1044	890 Deep pistachio
022	902 Deep garnet
381	938 Coffee brown
1011	948 Light peach
373	3045 Dark yellow-beige
874	3046 Medium yellow-beige
886	3047 Light yellow-beige
883	3064 True cocoa
292	3078 Pale topaz
382	3371 Black-brown
1048	3776 True mahogany
273	3787 Brown-gray
1098	3801 Watermelon
1066	3809 Dark turquoise
168	3810 True turquoise
1060	3811 Pale turquoise
100	3834 Dark grape
099	3835 Medium grape
090	3836 Light grape
347	3856 Pale mahogany
	5282 Metallic gold
HALF CROSS-STITCH (2X) (Stitch in direction of symbol)	
370	434 Medium caramel
1046	435 True caramel
362	437 Pale caramel
381	938 Coffee brown
BACKSTITCH (1X)	
351	400 Dark mahogany – fruit in basket
936	632 Deep cocoa – facial details, arms, hands, legs, feet
358	801 True coffee brown – hair of man in red robe and hair of woman at right
375	869 Dark hazel – front shepherd's sleeve and right side of gown
683	890 Deep pistachio – Joseph's cuffs, lower right shepherd's wrap
897	902 Deep Garnet – red robes
381	938 Coffee brown – all eyes, créche roof and stakes, Joseph and left shepherd's hair, Joseph's staff, shepherds' bags, leg band, manger
382	3371 Black-brown – brown shepherd robe, striped sash, staff and hair, donkey outline
904	3787 Brown-gray – all white collars, veils, blanket, sheep, lower right shepherd hair, basket
1068	3808 Deep turquoise – blue robe, Mary's blue gown
100	3834 Dark grape – lower right shepherd's robe
	5282 Metallic gold – star
STRAIGHT STITCH (1X)	
	5282 Metallic gold – halos and star

Stitch count: *134 high x 109 wide*
Finished design size:
28-count fabric – 9½ x 7¾ inches

Nativity

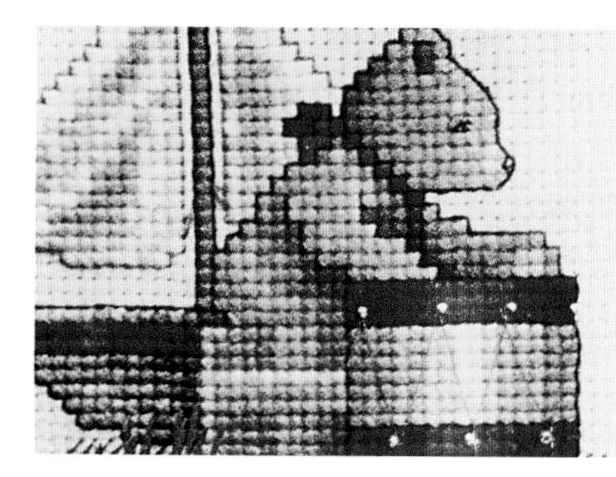

Santa, Rag Doll, and Teddy Bear Ornaments

Materials

For each ornament:

10" square of 14-count antique white Aida cloth
Cotton embroidery floss
Kreinik blending filament and cording
Mill Hill seed beads
4½"-diameter circle or 4¼×5½" oval of self-stick mounting board with foam
Crafts glue
½ yard of ¼"-wide red trim
6" length of ⅛"-wide red satin ribbon
4¼"-diameter circle or 4×5¼" oval of white felt

Instructions

Center and stitch the desired ornament chart from those at *right* and *opposite* on the Aida cloth. Use two plies of floss to work the stitches over one square of fabric unless otherwise specified. Attach the seed beads using two plies of matching floss. Press the stitched piece from the back.

Peel the protective paper backing from the mounting board. Center the foam side on the back of the stitched piece; press firmly to apply. Trim fabric to ½" beyond the edge of the mounting board. Fold fabric edges to the back of the board and glue in place.

Beginning at the bottom center of the ornament, glue the trim around the edge. Trim the excess. Fold the ribbon length in half to form a loop. Glue the ribbon ends to the center top on the ornament back. Glue the felt to the back. Let the glue dry.

Teddy Bear Ornament

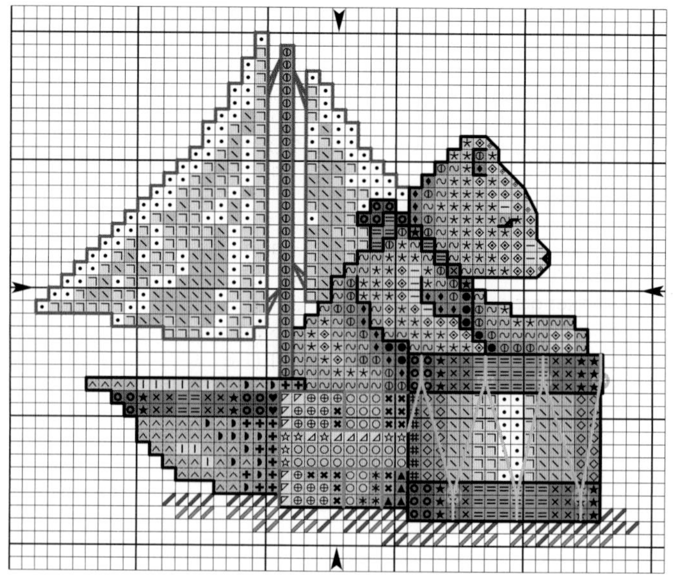

Teddy Bear Ornament Key

ANCHOR		DMC
CROSS-STITCH (2X)		
979	▲	312 Medium navy
013	★	321 True Christmas red
978	✖	322 Dark baby blue
977	⊕	334 Light navy
371	●	433 Dark caramel
370	♦	434 Medium caramel
1046	Ⓘ	435 True caramel
1045	∾	436 Light caramel
362	✯	437 Pale caramel
047	◘	498 Dark Christmas red
393	#	640 Medium beige-gray
392	◇	642 True beige-gray
391	◹	644 Light beige-gray
046	☒	666 Red
874	☆	676 Light old gold
885	◿	677 Pale old gold
890	✱	680 Dark old gold
891	○	729 Medium old gold
361	◈	738 Light tan
942	⊟	739 Pale tan
045	♥	814 Garnet
390	⌝	822 Pale beige-gray
817	✚	3345 Medium hunter green
267	◗	3346 True hunter green
266	∧	3347 Light hunter green
264	I	3348 Pale hunter green
140	◸	3755 True baby blue
1098	≡	3801 Watermelon
002	•	3865 Winter white

ANCHOR		DMC
HALF CROSS-STITCH (1X)		
393	/	640 Medium beige-gray – ground
1050	/	3781 Dark mocha – ground
BACKSTITCH (1X)		
979	/	312 Medium navy – top and left side of blue present
393	/	640 Medium beige-gray – sailboat
890	/	680 Dark old gold – gold ribbon of blue package
381	/	3031 Deep mocha – all other stitches
STRAIGHT STITCH WITH COUCHING (1X)		
	/	002C Kreinik gold cord – drum
MILL HILL SEED BEAD		
	⊗	40557 Gold – drum

Stitch count: *40 high x 47 wide*
Finished design size:
14-count fabric – 2⅞ x 3⅜ inches

Santa Ornament Key

ANCHOR DMC

CROSS-STITCH (2X)

013 ★ 321 True Christmas red
008 ⁚ 352 Light coral
006 ⁄ 353 Pale coral
047 ⊙ 498 Dark Christmas red
393 # 640 Medium beige-gray
392 ◇ 642 True beige-gray
391 ╲ 644 Light beige-gray
046 × 666 Red
336 II 758 Pale terra-cotta
045 ♥ 814 Garnet
390 ┐ 822 Pale beige-gray
1034 ◤ 931 Antique blue
1011 + 948 Peach
381 ■ 3031 Deep mocha
883 S 3064 True cocoa
267 ◗ 3346 True hunter green
266 ^ 3347 Light hunter green
050 ♡ 3708 Geranium
1010 □ 3770 Blush
1007 ⊖ 3772 Dark cocoa
1050 ◆ 3781 Dark mocha
1098 = 3801 Watermelon
002 • 3865 Winter white

ANCHOR DMC

BLENDED NEEDLE CROSS-STITCH

885 ⧄ 677 Pale old gold (2X) and 002 Kreinik gold blending filament (1X)
891 ⊞ 729 Medium old gold (2X) and 002 Kreinik gold blending filament (1X)

BACKSTITCH (1X)

338 ╱ 356 True terra-cotta – sides of Santa's face, portion of nose
936 ╱ 632 Deep cocoa – bottom of Santa's nose
381 ╱ 3031 Deep mocha – all other stitches

STRAIGHT STITCH (1X)

235 ╱ 414 Steel – Santa's eyebrows

FRENCH KNOT (1X)

1098 ● 3801 Watermelon – berries

Stitch count: *53 high x 41 wide*

Finished design size:
14-count fabric – 3 3/4 x 3 inches

Santa Ornament

Rag Doll Ornament

Rag Doll Ornament Key

ANCHOR DMC

CROSS-STITCH (2X)

400 ▷ 317 True charcoal
013 ★ 321 True Christmas red
858 ⁄ 353 Coral
401 ■ 413 Medium charcoal
047 ⊙ 498 Dark Christmas red
393 # 640 Medium beige-gray
392 ◇ 642 True beige-gray
391 ╲ 644 Light beige-gray
046 × 666 Red
874 ☆ 676 Light old gold
890 ✳ 680 Dark old gold
891 ○ 729 Medium old gold
336 II 758 Pale terra-cotta
045 ♥ 814 Garnet
390 ┐ 822 Pale beige-gray
1011 + 948 Peach
267 ◗ 3346 True hunter green
266 ^ 3347 Light hunter green
264 I 3348 Pale hunter green
1098 = 3801 Watermelon
002 • 3865 Winter white

ANCHOR DMC

HALF CROSS-STITCH (2X)

393 ╱ 640 Medium beige-gray
1050 ╱ 3781 Dark mocha

BACKSTITCH (1X)

338 ╱ 356 True terra-cotta – face, mouth, hand
370 ╱ 434 Caramel – eyebrows
393 ╱ 640 Medium beige-gray – pinafore
1098 ╱ 3801 Watermelon – nose
381 ╱ 3031 Deep mocha – all other stitches

STRAIGHT STITCH (1X)

1005 ╱ 498 Dark Christmas red – hair

FRENCH KNOT (1X wrapped once)

874 ● 676 Light old gold – dress buttons

MILL HILL BEAD

⊗ 02014 Black – eyes

Stitch count: *38 high x 45 wide*

Finished design size:
14-count fabric – 2 3/4 x 3 1/4 inches

Nostalgic Santa

Materials

For the stocking: 15×22" piece of 25-count raw Dublin linen

For framed piece: 25-count raw Dublin linen measuring 8" larger than each dimension of the frame opening

Cotton embroidery floss

Kreinik blending filament and cording

Mill Hill beads

Erasable fabric marker

11×18" piece of fusible fleece

5/8 yard of red crinkle fabric

1/4 yard of red quilted fabric

1 1/4 yards of 1/4"-diameter cording

Matching sewing thread

Instructions

Center and stitch the Nostalgic Santa chart on *pages 20–21* on the fabric. Use three plies of floss to work the stitches over two threads of fabric unless specified. Attach beads with two plies of floss. Press the piece from the back.

Center and fuse the fleece to the back of the stitched piece, following the manufacturer's instructions. Use the erasable fabric marker to draw the stocking outline as indicated by the dashed line on the chart. Cut out the stocking shape 1/2" beyond the marked outline.

Use the trimmed stitched piece as a pattern to cut a matching back and two lining pieces from the red crinkle fabric. From the remaining red crinkle fabric, cut a 2×7" hanging strip and enough 1 3/4"-wide bias strips to make a 45" length of piping. From the red quilted fabric, cut a 9×14" rectangle for the cuff.

Sew the short ends of the 1 3/4"-wide bias strips together to make a continuous length. Center the cording lengthwise on the wrong side of the piping strip. Fold the fabric around the cording, long edges even. Use a zipper foot to sew through both layers, close to the cording.

With raw edges even and using a zipper foot, baste piping around the sides and foot of the stocking front. Sew the stocking front to the back, right sides together, along the basting lines, leaving the top straight edge open. Trim the seams and clip the curves. Turn right side out; press.

With right sides facing, sew the lining pieces together with 1/2" seams, leaving the top edge open. Trim the seams and clip the curves; do not turn. Slip the lining inside the stocking, wrong sides together. Baste the top edges of the stocking and lining together.

For the hanger, press under 1/2" along each long edge of the hanging strip. Fold the strip in half lengthwise, aligning pressed edges; press again. Sew the long edges together opposite the fold. Fold the strip in half to form a loop. Baste the ends to the top inner corner on the heel side of the stocking with the loop inside the stocking.

For the cuff, sew the short edges of the 9×14" rectangle together to form a circle; press the seams open. Press the cuff in half lengthwise, wrong sides together, matching raw edges and seams. Slip the cuff into the stocking, raw edges even, aligning the cuff and the center back seams. Sew the cuff to the stocking. Zigzag-stitch or overcast the raw edges together. Fold the cuff over to the outside of the stocking.

For a framed piece, stitch the desired portion of the Nostalgic Santa chart in the same manner as stocking.

Snow Angel Blessings Ornament

Materials

9" square of 18-count ivory Aida cloth

Cotton embroidery floss

3 3/4"-diameter circle of self-stick mounting board with foam

Thick white crafts glue

15" length of purchased pale pink sew-in piping

7" length of 1/8"-wide pale pink satin ribbon

3 3/4"-diameter circle of ivory felt

Instructions

Center and stitch the angel from the Snow Angel Blessings chart on *page 22* on the Aida cloth. Use two plies of floss to work the stitches over one square of fabric unless specified. Press the piece from the back.

Peel the protective paper from the mounting board. Center the foam side on the back of the stitched piece; press firmly to apply. Trim the fabric to 1/2" beyond the edge of the mounting board. Fold the edges to the back; glue.

Beginning at the bottom center of the ornament, glue the piping around the edges on the ornament back. Trim the excess. Fold the ribbon length in half, forming a hanging loop. Glue the ribbon ends to the center top on the ornament back. Center and glue the felt to the back. Let dry.

Snow Angel Blessings

Materials

16×14" piece of 32-count ice blue Belfast linen
Cotton embroidery floss
Desired frame

Instructions

Center and stitch the Snow Angel Blessings chart on *page 22* on the fabric. Use two plies of floss to work the stitches over two threads of fabric unless otherwise specified. Press the stitched piece from the back. Frame as desired.

Tree Place Mat

Materials

13×18" piece of 28-count lambswool Jobelan fabric
Matching sewing thread
Cotton embroidery floss

Instructions

Before stitching, machine-topstitch ½" from the outer edges of the Jobelan fabric. Begin stitching the bottom left corner of the tree motif from the Patchwork Cardinal Tray chart on *pages 24–25* in one corner of the fabric, 1" in from the topstitching. Use three plies of floss to work the stitches over two threads of the fabric unless otherwise specified. When stitching is complete, remove the fabric threads between the raw edges and the topstitching to fringe. Press the finished piece from the back.

Nostalgic Santa Key

ANCHOR	DMC
CROSS-STITCH (3X)	
979	312 Medium navy
013	321 True Christmas red
978	322 Dark baby blue
977	334 Light navy
008	352 Coral
858	353 Pale peach
371	433 Dark caramel
370	434 Medium caramel
1046	435 True caramel
1045	436 Light caramel
362	437 Pale caramel
047	498 Dark Christmas red
889	610 Deep drab brown
856	611 Deep pecan
854	612 Medium drab brown
852	613 Pale pecan
393	640 Medium beige-gray
392	642 True beige-gray
391	644 Light beige-gray
900	648 Light beaver gray
046	666 Red
874	676 Light old gold
885	677 Pale old gold
890	680 Dark old gold
891	729 Medium old gold
361	738 Light tan
942	739 Pale tan
336	758 Pale terra-cotta
045	814 Garnet
390	822 Pale beige-gray
1034	931 Antique blue
1011	948 Light peach
381	3031 Deep mocha
883	3064 True cocoa
397	3072 Pale beaver gray
268	3345 Medium hunter green
267	3346 True hunter green
266	3347 Light hunter green
264	3348 Pale hunter green
050	3708 Geranium
140	3755 True baby blue
1010	3770 Blush
1007	3772 Dark cocoa
1050	3781 Dark mocha
1098	3801 Watermelon
002	3865 Winter white
BLENDED NEEDLE CROSS-STITCH	
885	677 Pale old gold (3X) and 002 Kreinik gold blending filament (2X)
890	680 Dark old gold (3X) and 002 Kreinik gold blending filament (2X)
306	729 Medium old gold (3X) and 002 Kreinik gold blending filament (2X)
BACKSTITCH (1X)	
979	312 Medium navy – doll in blue dress and bows, blue package behind rag doll
338	356 True terra-cotta – side of Santa's face, portion of his nose, dolls: arms, hands, faces, mouths and the nose of doll in blue
235	414 Steel – Santa's eyebrows
370	434 Medium caramel – eyebrows of doll in blue and rag doll
047	498 Dark Christmas red – rag doll hair, green package at toe
936	632 Deep cocoa – Santa's nose
393	640 Medium beige-gray – rag doll pinafore, sailboat
890	680 Dark old gold – ribbon on blue packages
1098	3801 Watermelon – rag doll nose
381	3031 Deep mocha – all other stitches
STRAIGHT STITCH (1X)	
	002 Kreinik gold blending filament – drum, green package
	102 Kreinik Vatican gold blending filament – green package
FRENCH KNOT	
874	676 Light old gold – rag doll buttons (1X)
1098	3801 Watermelon – berries (2X)
MILL HILL BEAD	
	02014 Black – rag doll eyes
	40557 Gold – drum

Stitch count: *206 high x 116 wide*

Finished design size:
25-count fabric – 16⅜ x 9¼ inches

Nostalgic Santa Stocking

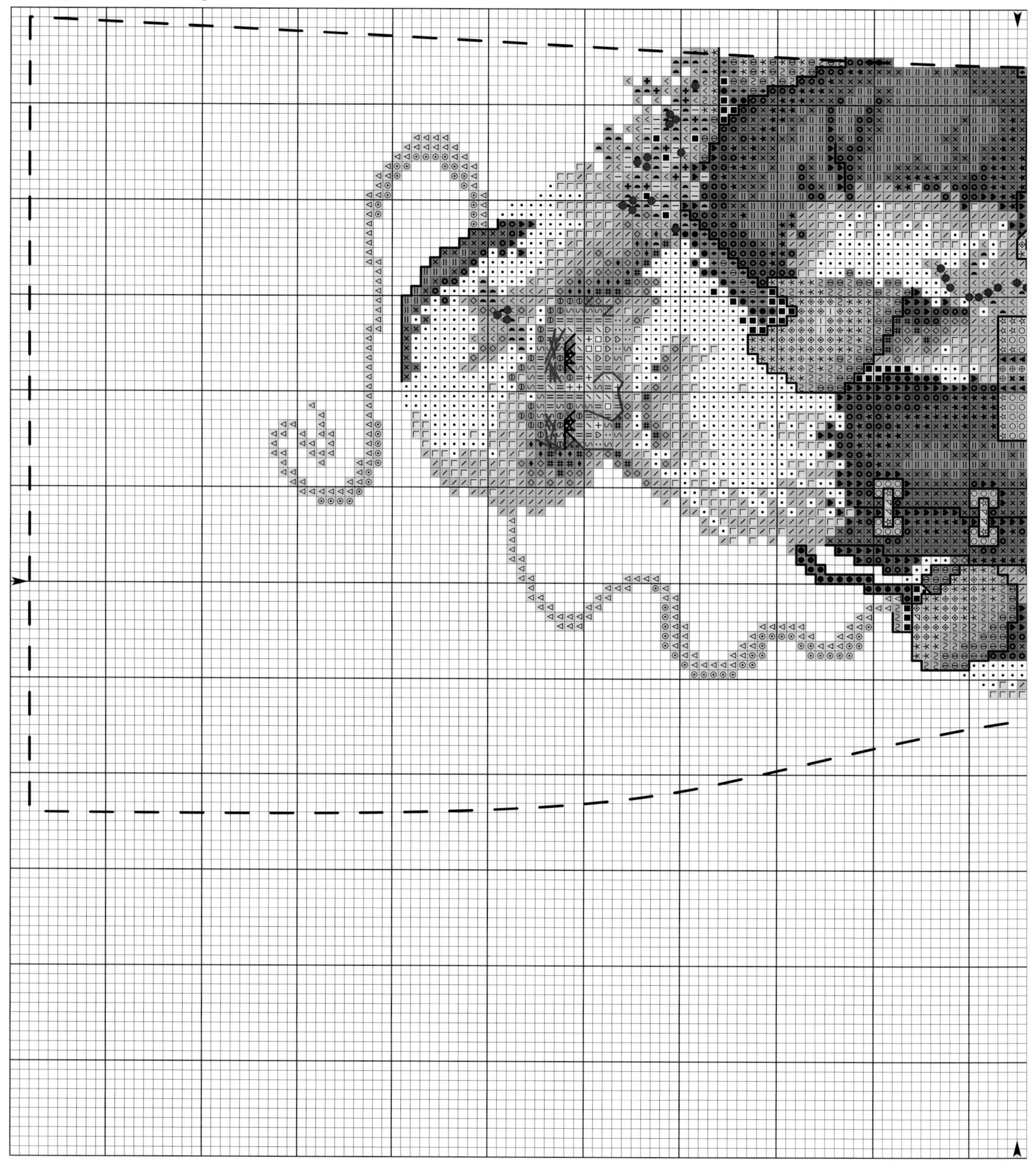

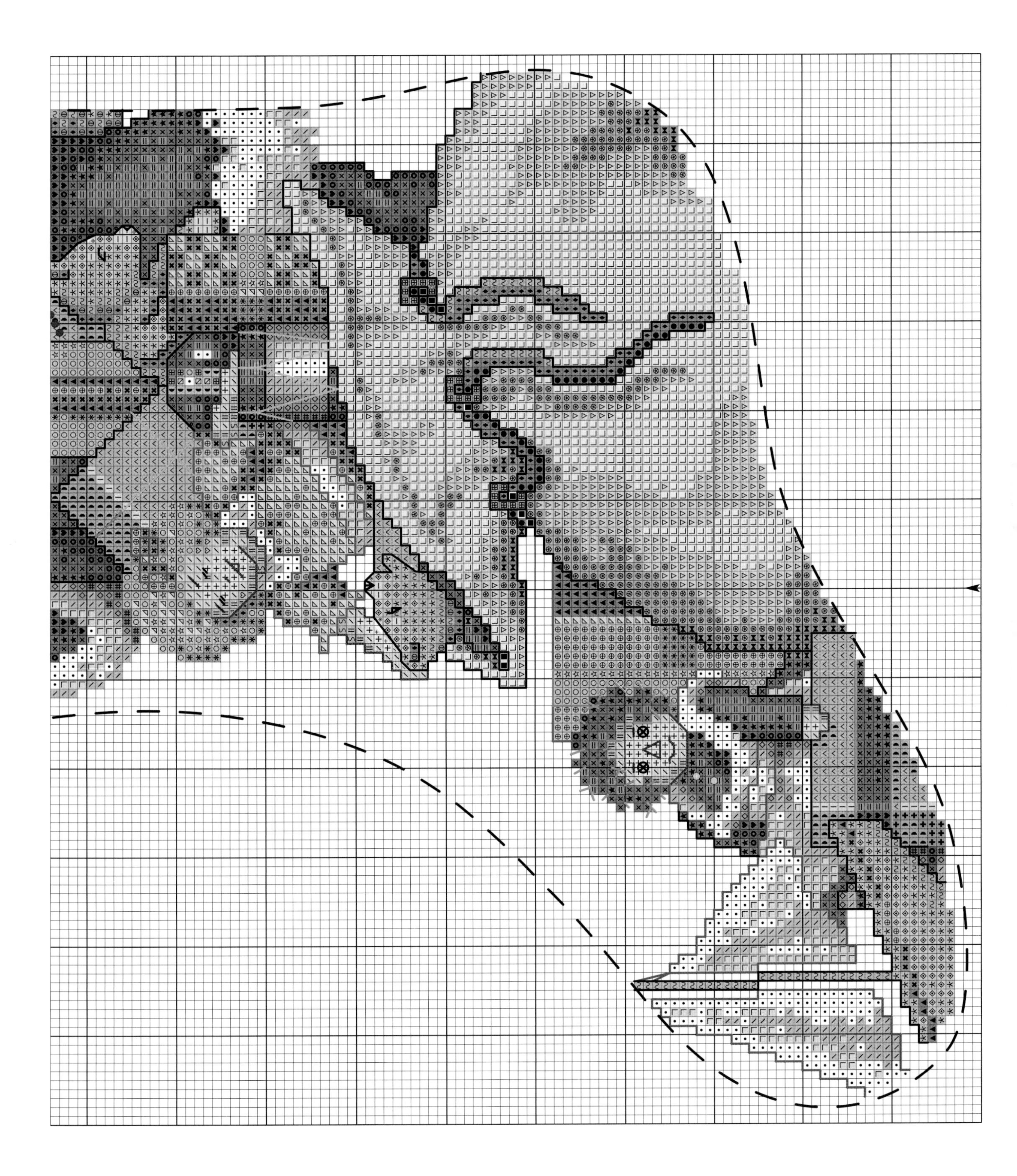

Snow Angel Blessings

Snow Angel Blessings Key

ANCHOR DMC

CROSS-STITCH (2X)

ANCHOR	Symbol	DMC
002	•	000 White
001	☆	B5200 Bright white
895	O	223 Medium shell pink
893	+	224 Light shell pink
892	−	225 Pale shell pink
969	▽	316 Medium antique mauve
1047	◘	402 Mahogany
879	▲	501 Dark blue-green
876	×	503 True blue-green
1042	╲	504 Pale blue-green
1041	■	535 Ash gray
874	□	676 Light old gold
885	I	677 Pale old gold
306	✱	729 Medium old gold
275	:	746 Off-white
234	^	762 Pearl gray
1016	S	778 Pale antique mauve
390	=	822 Beige-gray
868	♡	3779 Pale rosewood
216	⊙	3816 True celadon green

HALF CROSS-STITCH (2X)
(stitch in direction of symbol)

001 ╲ B5200 Bright white

BACKSTITCH (1X)

879 / 501 Dark blue-green – vines

890 / 680 Dark old gold – halo

1041 / 535 Ash gray – all other stitches

FRENCH KNOT (1X wrapped twice)

1041 ● 535 Ash gray – above “i”

LAZY DAISY (1X)

1041 0 535 Ash gray – stars on string

RUNNING STITCH (1X)

1041 — — 535 Ash gray – wings

Stitch count: *101 high x 81 wide*

Finished design size:
32-count fabric – 6 1/3 x 5 inches

Snowflake Place Card

Materials

7" square of 28-count lambswool Jobelan fabric
Cotton embroidery floss
Computer and color printer
Light green patterned scrapbook paper
Brown suede scrapbook paper
Straight- and decorative-edge scissors
Crafts glue

Instructions

Center and stitch the snowflake motif from the Patchwork Cardinal Tray chart on *pages 24–25* on the Jobelan fabric. Use one ply of floss to work the cross-stitches over one thread of the fabric. Use one ply of Black-brown (DMC 3371) floss to sew running stitches four threads beyond the outermost stitches of the snowflake, creating a square. Press the stitched piece from the back.

Trim the stitched piece a scant 1/4" beyond the running stitched square. To fringe, remove the fabric threads beginning at the raw edges and stopping one thread from the square.

On a computer, type the desired name using a 2" left margin. Print a test sample. Adjust the font size to fit the name in a space approximately 2" wide. When satisfied, print the name in dark green ink on the light green patterned scrapbook paper. Trim the printed sheet into a 4 1/8×2 1/8" rectangle, centering the text in the right half of the rectangle about 2" from the left edge.

Mount the printed rectangle on the right side of the brown suede scrapbook paper. Use decorative-edge scissors to trim the brown suede paper 1/8" beyond the edges of the printed rectangle. Mount the decorative-edge suede rectangle on the wrong side of the brown suede paper. Use a straight-edge scissors to trim the paper 1/8" beyond the edges of the decorative-edge rectangle. Mount the stitched piece onto the place-card front.

Star Napkin

Materials

16" square of 28-count lambswool Jobelan fabric
Matching sewing thread
Cotton embroidery floss

Instructions

Before stitching, work a line of machine-topstitching 1/2" from the outer edges of the Jobelan fabric. Use sewing thread to base a 2 1/4×2 3/4" rectangle in one corner of the napkin 1" in from the topstitching. Center and stitch the checked star motif from the Patchwork Cardinal Tray chart on *pages 24–25* in the basted rectangle. Use three plies of floss to work the stitches over two threads of the fabric unless otherwise specified. When stitching is complete, remove the fabric threads between the raw edges and the topstitching. Remove the basting thread and press from the back.

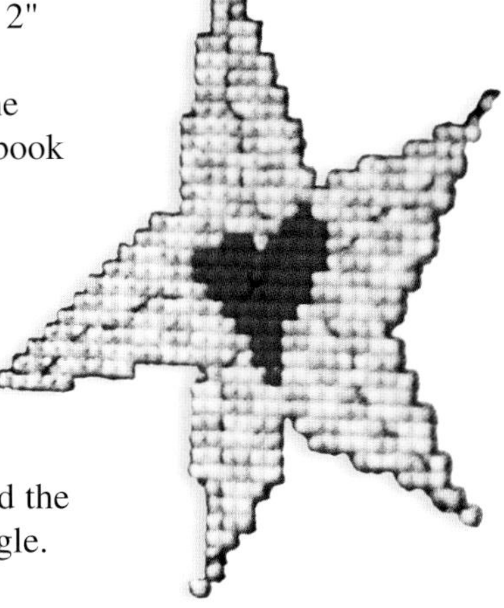

Patchwork Cardinal Tray

Materials

16" square of 28-count lambswool Jobelan fabric
Cotton embroidery floss
12" square piece of fleece
Purchased 12" square wood tray (Sudberry #60131)
Spray adhesive

Instructions

Center and stitch the Patchwork Cardinal Tray chart at *right* on the Jobelan fabric. Use two plies of floss to work the stitches over two threads of the fabric unless otherwise specified. Press the stitched piece from the back.

Cut the fleece the same size as the mounting board from the tray. Spray the board lightly with adhesive and position the fleece on top. Center the wrong side of the stitchery over the fleece on the board; tape the edges to the back. Insert the design into the tray. Reassemble the tray following the manufacturer's instructions.

Symbols of the season

Patchwork Cardinal Tray Key

ANCHOR DMC
CROSS-STITCH (2X)

ANCHOR	Symbol	DMC
002	•	000 White
218	◆	319 Pistachio
374	○	420 Medium hazel
372	I	422 Light hazel
1046	⧄	435 True caramel
267	×	469 Dark avocado
265	–	471 Light avocado
358	▲	801 Coffee brown
045	●	814 Dark garnet
1005	+	816 Light garnet
382	■	3371 Black-brown
305	▽	3821 Straw

BACKSTITCH (1X)
382 / 3371 Black-brown

STRAIGHT STITCH (1X)
382 / 3371 Black-brown – berries, bird's eye and heart on star

Stitch count: *151 high x 151 wide*

Finished design size:
14-count fabric – 10¾ x 10¾ inches

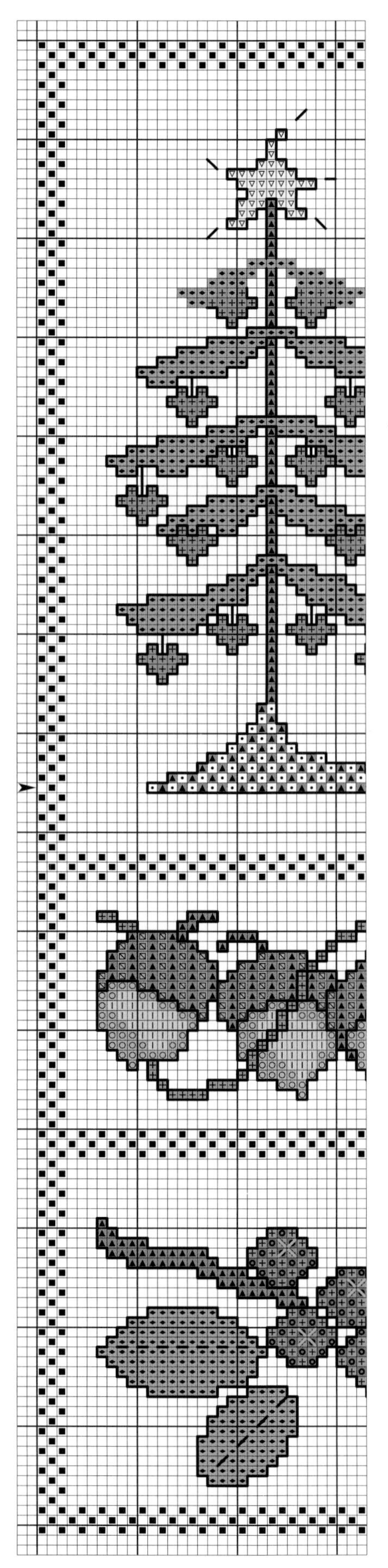

Deck the Halls

We all like to dress up for holiday gatherings. Why shouldn't we do the same for our homes? Whether your taste is elegant or casual, or something in between, we've assembled designs to dress your home in festive style. Why not begin your decorating with this clever ornament box tray at *left?* Its colorful trims and a surprise guest capture the excitement of trimming the tree as boxes are opened to reveal long-stored treasures.

Project instructions begin on page 50.

Design: Louise Young • Photography: Hopkins Associates

Deck
the Halls

If you prefer the formal elegance of traditional table settings, this classic design will blend beautifully with your dinnerware pieces. The colorful fruit-and-holly motif wraps gracefully around each end of the table runner at *left.*

Stitch a single motif from the Della Robbia Table Runner over one thread of fabric to make coordinating napkins. Napkin rings also can be fashioned from leftover scraps of fabric and a cardboard tube.

Apply a painted crackle finish to purchased wooden candleholders. Choose a motif from the table runner to stitch over one thread of fabric to create a one-of-a-kind decorative accent, *above.*

Project instructions begin on page 35.

Design: Barbara Sestok • Photography: Greg Scheidemann

merry christmas!
abcdefghijklmnop
qrstuvwxyz
1234567890

Snow falls gently on the tiny home nestled among the stately pines on this cheery holiday sampler *opposite.* The tranquil images worked in stitches are certain to warm your home and spirits. The reindeer, snowflakes, and other classic Christmas motifs also can be used to create additional items for yourself or to give as gifts.

Project instructions begin on page 40.
Design: Robin Clark • Photography: Scott Little

A simple glass hurricane filled with colorful ornaments takes center stage when you dress it for the holidays, *right.* A timeless message of the season is stitched in sparkling metallic threads and accented with glittering seed beads to make an elegant statement.

Project instructions begin on page 40.
Design: Vicki Schofield • Photography: Hopkins Associates

Deck the Halls

A plain papier-mâché box is easily transformed into a fabulous holiday centerpiece, *opposite.* Simply wrap the sides of the box and lid with rectangles of stitched fabric. Then fill with flowers and greens. For fresh flowers, line the box with a small dish.

Project instructions begin on page 44.

Design: Kathy Zeitman • Photography: Dean Tanner

Nothing says Christmas like a serving tray, *below,* dressed in the lively reds and greens of the season. The contemporary style of this handsome poinsettia design will complement both casual and formal dinnerware.

Project instructions begin on page 44.

Design: Kathy Zeitman • Photography: Dean Tanner

A familiar holiday image is given a contemporary twist in the elegant pillow shown *above.* The size and shape of the pillow can be changed easily by stitching the chart more than once. Because the design is worked in whole stitches, it also can be easily converted to needlepoint by adding a solid color for the background.

Project instructions begin on page 45.

Design: Kathy Zeitman • Photography: Dean Tanner

Della Robbia Table Runner

Materials

17×55" piece of 28-count cameo peach Jobelan fabric
Cotton embroidery floss
17×54" piece of fusible fleece
Erasable fabric marker
½ yard of beige cotton fabric
½ yard of burgundy cotton fabric
3¼ yards of ¼"-diameter cording
Matching sewing threads

Instructions

Find the center of one short edge of the Jobelan fabric and measure up 3". Begin stitching the center bottom of the Della Robbia Table Runner chart on *pages 36–37* there. Use two plies of floss to work the stitches over two threads of the fabric unless otherwise specified. Repeat the design on the opposite end of the fabric in the same manner. Press the stitched piece from the back.

Center and fuse the fleece to the back of the stitched fabric, following the manufacturer's instructions. Trim 1" from each long edge of the stitched piece to center the design on a 15" width of fabric. Use the erasable fabric marker to draw a smooth curved line from long edge to long edge at one end of the stitched piece about 2" beyond the outermost stitches. Cut on the drawn line. Repeat for the opposite end.

Use the trimmed stitched piece as a pattern to cut a matching back from the beige fabric. From the burgundy fabric, cut enough 1¾"-wide bias strips to make a 118" length of piping.

Sew the short ends of the 1¾"-wide bias strips together to make a continuous length. Center the cording lengthwise on the wrong side of the piping strip. Fold the fabric around the cording, long edges even. Use a zipper foot to sew through both layers, close to the cording.

With raw edges even and using a zipper foot, baste the piping around the perimeter of the table runner front. Right sides together, sew the table runner front to the back along the basting lines, leaving an opening on one long edge for turning. Trim the seams and clip the curves. Turn the table runner right side out; press. Slip-stitch the opening closed.

Della Robbia Table Runner Key

ANCHOR	DMC
CROSS-STITCH (2X)	
020	221 Deep shell pink
019	304 Christmas red
1025	347 Salmon
858	353 Peach
879	501 Dark blue-green
877	502 Medium blue-green
046	666 Red
323	722 Bittersweet
302	743 True yellow
300	745 Light yellow
309	781 Christmas gold
1005	816 Garnet
359	898 Coffee brown
334	900 Burnt orange
340	919 Copper
861	935 Pine green
298	972 Tangerine
246	986 Forest green
859	3053 Gray-green
266	3347 Light hunter green
264	3348 Pale hunter green
261	3363 Loden
1027	3722 True shell pink
1007	3772 Cocoa
875	3813 Light blue-green
891	3822 Light straw
100	3834 Dark grape
099	3835 Medium grape
090	3836 Light grape
308	3852 Deep straw
1003	3853 Autumn gold
944	3862 Mocha-beige
BACKSTITCH (1X)	
382	3371 Black-brown

Stitch count: *152 high x 227 wide*
Finished design size:
28-count fabric – 10¼ x 16¼ inches

Dellia Robbia Table Runner

Pear Napkin

Materials

17" square of 28-count cameo peach Jobelan fabric
Matching and contrasting sewing thread
Cotton embroidery floss

Instructions

Before stitching, press under 1/4" twice on all edges of the Jobelan fabric, mitering the corners. Topstitch 3/16" from the pressed edges with matching sewing thread.

Use contrasting sewing thread to baste a 2½" square in one corner of the napkin 1" in from the pressed edges. Center and stitch the design from the Pear Napkin chart *opposite, right* in the basted square. Use two plies of floss to work the cross-stitches over two threads of the fabric. Backstitch with one ply of floss. When stitching is complete, remove the basting thread and press the finished napkin from the back.

Holly Napkin Ring

Materials

7½×7" piece of 28-count cameo peach Jobelan fabric
Cotton embroidery floss
½" length of cardboard paper towel tube
Sheet of off-white soft crafts foam
Spray adhesive
Purchased red sew-in narrow piping
Crafts glue
Off-white felt

Instructions

Center and stitch the design from the Holly Napkin Ring chart *opposite, top right* on the Jobelan fabric. Use one ply of floss to work the cross-stitches over one thread of the fabric. Backstitch with one ply of floss. Press the stitched piece from the back.

Cut a 1½"-wide strip of crafts foam to wrap around the cardboard tube. Spray a coat of adhesive on one side of the foam. Immediately press the adhesive side of the foam onto the outside surface of the cardboard tube, matching the short edges.

Centering the design, trim the stitched piece into a 7½×2½" rectangle. Press under ½" at one short edge of the stitched piece. Wrap the stitched piece around the outside of the foam-covered tube, centering the design and overlapping the remaining short edge with the pressed edge. Glue the pressed edge in place. Fold the long edges of the fabric to the inside of the tube and glue in place to secure.

Glue the piping around the top and bottom edges on the inside of the napkin ring. Cut a 1½"-wide strip of felt to fit inside of napkin ring and glue in place.

Della Robbia Candleholder

Materials

Tape measure
Purchased wood candleholder with square base
Fine-grit sandpaper
Acrylic paints: antique white, metallic gold
Crackle finish
Sponge brushes
28-count cameo peach Jobelan fabric 1" wider and taller than the distance needed to wrap around the candleholders
Contrasting and matching sewing thread
Cotton embroidery floss
Purchased red sew-in piping
Crafts glue

Instructions

Sand all surfaces of the candleholders with fine-grit sandpaper. Remove the sanding dust with a clean cloth. Use a sponge brush to apply two coats of gold paint to all surfaces of the candleholders, allowing the paint to dry after each coat and sanding before applying the next coat.

Following the manufacturer's instructions, use a sponge brush to apply a coat of crackle finish to the candleholders. When the first coat is dry, use the sponge brush to apply a coat of antique white paint to the candleholders.

Use the tape measure to measure the distance around the base of each candleholder. Add 1" to this measurement for overlap and cut a 7"-wide strip of Jobelan fabric. Fold the fabric in half and hand-baste a line along the fold with contrasting sewing thread to indicate one corner of the base. Measure one side of the base. Use this measurement to baste a line representing each corner of the base, dividing the fabric into four equal sections with an extra ½" at each end for overlap.

Note: Your measurements may vary from those given above depending on the style of candleholder used.

Center and stitch the Candleholder chart *opposite, left* within each section. Use one ply of floss to work the stitches over one thread of the fabric. Backstitch with one ply of floss. When stitching is complete, remove the basting thread and press the stitched piece from the back.

Referring to the photographs on *pages 29 and 39,* glue piping along the top and bottom edges of the base. Fold under the long edges of the stitched piece to fit between the piping, centering the designs; press.

Trim the excess fabric from the long edges, leaving a ½" seam allowance. Press under ½" at one short edge. Wrap the piece around the base, centering a design on each side of the base. Overlap the remaining short edge with the pressed edge. Slip-stitch in place.

TIP
perfect rounded corners

There are several ways to make perfectly rounded corners like those on the Della Robbia Table Runner on *pages 28–29.* First, determine the radius of the arc by folding the fabric lengthwise. For a half circle like the one shown, fold the fabric in half. If you prefer a straight span of fabric between the arches, fold the fabric off center. Place the fabric on a pinnable mat or old magazine.

Measure and mark the distance from the fold to the side edge of the fabric. Measure the same distance from the tip of the fold. The point where the two distances meet will be the center of the arc. To mark the arc, use a piece of string and an erasable marker (for smaller projects use a compass). Tie the string firmly around the barrel of the marker, just above the point. Position the point of the marker on the side edge of the fabric. Holding the marker in that position, pull the thread taut with the opposite end over the marked point on the fabric. Fasten the string to the mat with a thumbtack or straight pin. Move the point of the marker across the fabric to the top of the fabric (see diagram *below*). Another method that works for smaller projects is tracing the curve of a dinner plate or large platter with an erasable marker.

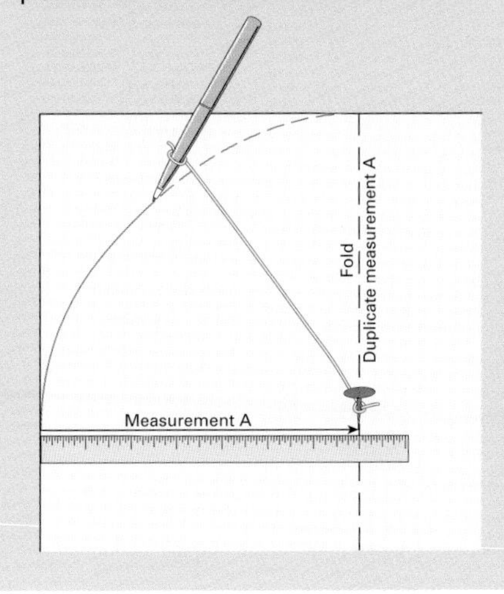

Holly Napkin Ring Key

ANCHOR		DMC
CROSS-STITCH (2X)		
020	♦	221 Deep shell pink
1025	⊞	347 Salmon
879	✚	501 Dark blue-green
877	#	502 Medium blue-green
1005	★	816 Garnet
1027	ǁ	3722 Medium shell pink
875	⊖	3813 Light blue-green
BACKSTITCH (1X)		
382	/	3371 Black-brown

Stitch count: *18 high x 32 wide*

Finished design size:
28-count fabric (over 1 thread) – 2/3 x 1 1/8 inches

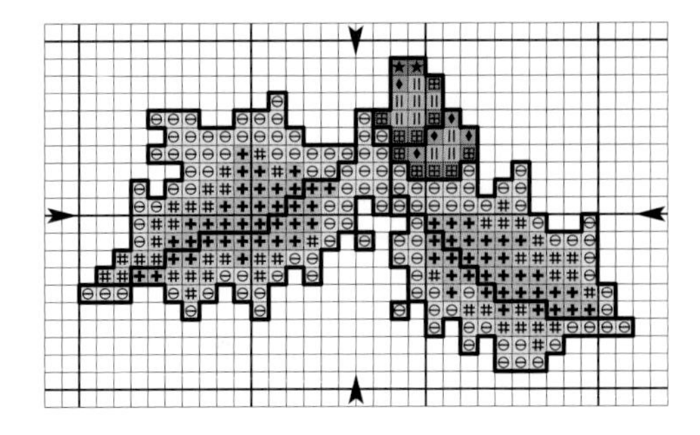

Candleholder

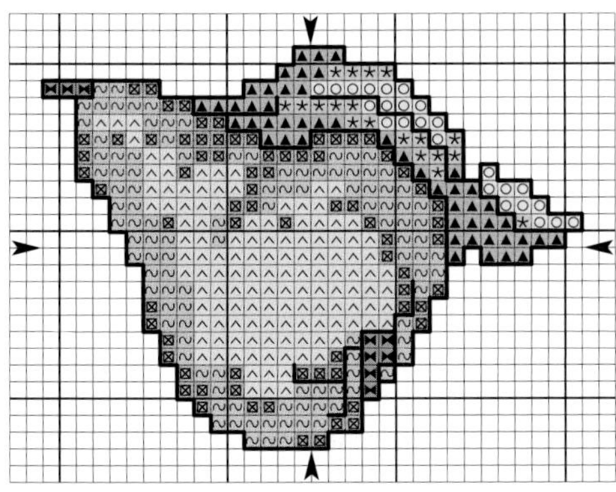

Pear Napkin

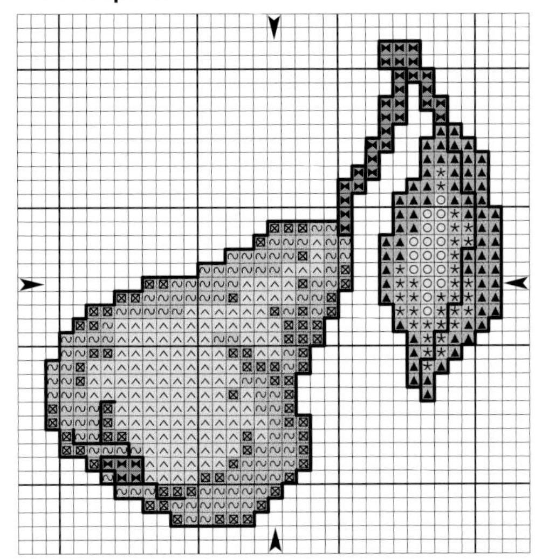

Pear Napkin and Candleholder Key

ANCHOR		DMC
CROSS-STITCH (2X)		
309	⊠	781 Christmas gold
340	⧓	919 Copper
246	▲	986 Forest green
266	✶	3347 Light hunter green
264	○	3348 Pale hunter green
891	^	3822 Light straw
308	∿	3852 Deep straw
BACKSTITCH (1X)		
382	/	3371 Black-brown

Napkin stitch count:
35 high x 33 wide

Napkin finished design size:
28-count fabric – 2 1/2 x 2 1/3 inches

Candleholder stitch count:
24 high x 32 wide

Candleholder finished design size:
28-count fabric (over 1 thread) – 7/8 x 1 1/8 inches

Christmas Sampler

Materials

13×18" piece of 14-count beige Aida cloth
Cotton embroidery floss
Desired frame

Instructions

Center and stitch the Home for Christmas Sampler chart on *pages 42–43* on the fabric. Use two plies of floss to work the stitches over one square of the fabric unless otherwise specified. Work the remaining stitches as specified in the key. Press the finished piece from the back. Frame the piece as desired.

Peace Hurricane

Materials

10×11" piece of 28-count raw Glasgow linen
Needle Necessities overdyed floss
Kreinik #4 very fine braid
Cotton embroidery floss
Mill Hill seed beads
7×8" piece of Christmas-print cotton fabric
24" length of ½"-wide gold trim
Purchased 24"-long twisted cording tie with tassels
Matching sewing thread
11½"-tall glass hurricane measuring 17" in circumference

Instructions

Center and stitch the Peace Hurricane chart *opposite* on the linen. Use two plies of overdyed floss or one strand of braid to work the stitches over two threads of the fabric unless otherwise specified. When working with overdyed floss, complete each cross-stitch before beginning the next. Use one ply of floss to cross-stitch "Peace" over one fabric thread. Refer to the diagrams to work the remaining stitches. Attach the seed beads using two plies of matching floss. Press the stitched piece from the back.

Trim the stitched piece ¾" beyond the outermost stitches. Use the trimmed stitched piece as a pattern to cut a matching shape from the Christmas-print fabric for the back.

Baste the straight edge of the trim ½" from the raw edges on the front of the stitched piece. Sew the front and back together with right sides facing, leaving an opening on the top edge for turning. Trim the seams and clip the corners. Turn right side out and press. Slip-stitch the opening closed.

Beginning with the center of the cording, tie at the center bottom of the piece, hand-sew the tie to the bottom and side edges on the front of the ornament. Tie the piece around the glass hurricane.

Peace Hurricane Key

CROSS-STITCH (over 2 threads)

- 153 Needle Necessities Razzle Dazzle red (2X)
- 002 Kreinik gold #4 braid (1X)

CROSS-STITCH (1X over 1 thread)

- 304 DMC Christmas red

SMYRNA CROSS VARIATION

- 153 Needle Necessities Razzle Dazzle red (2X) and 002 Kreinik gold #4 braid (1X)

LAYERED HERRINGBONE

- 153 Needle Necessities Overdyed Floss (2X) and 002 Kreinik gold metallic #4 braid (1X)

MILL HILL BEAD

- 03049 Red
- 00557 Gold

Stitch count: *67 high x 54 wide*

Finished design size:
28-count fabric – 4 3/4 x 3 7/8 inches

Peace Hurricane

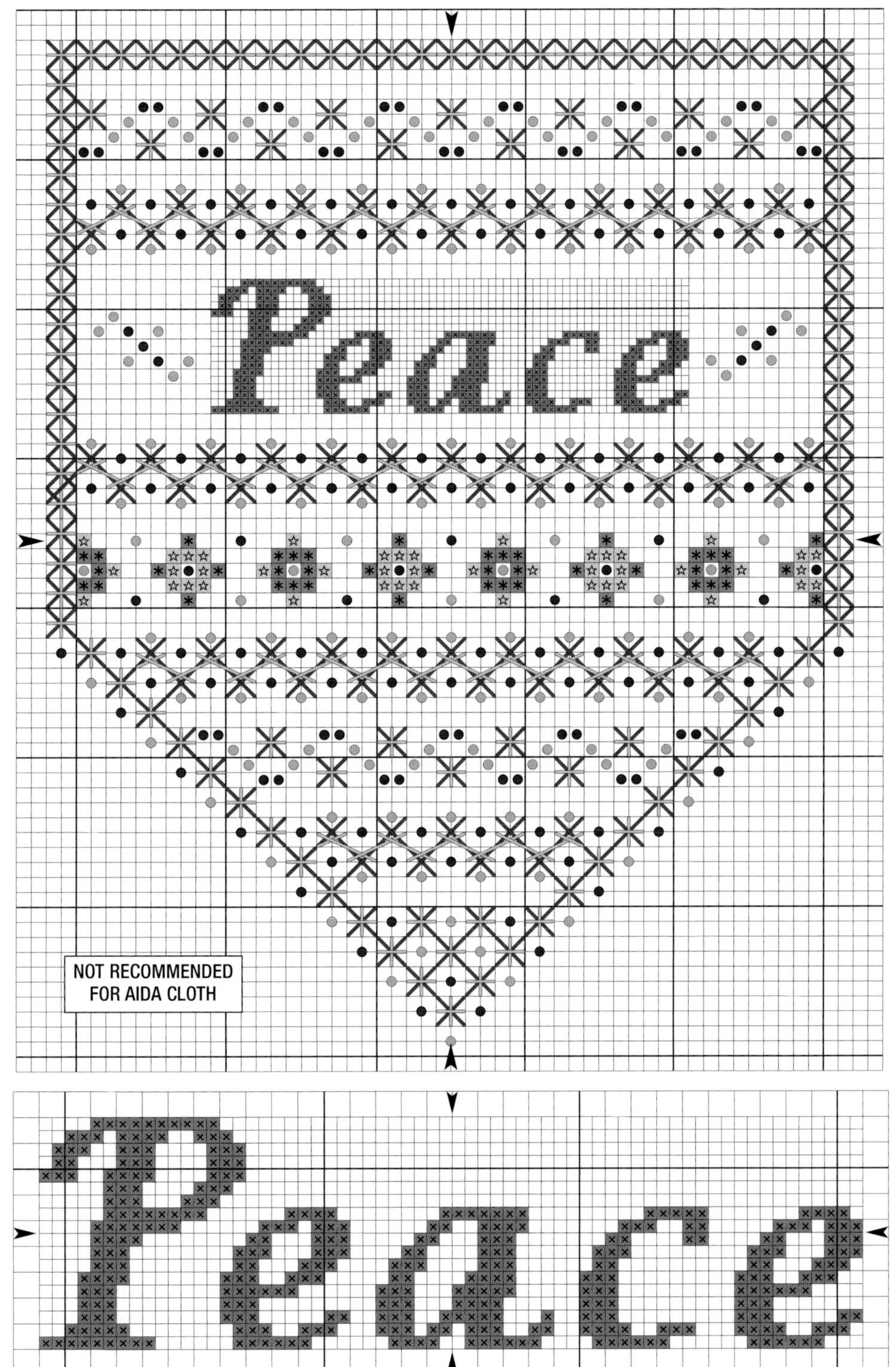

Petite Cross-Stitch (work over one thread of fabric)

TIPS

color options

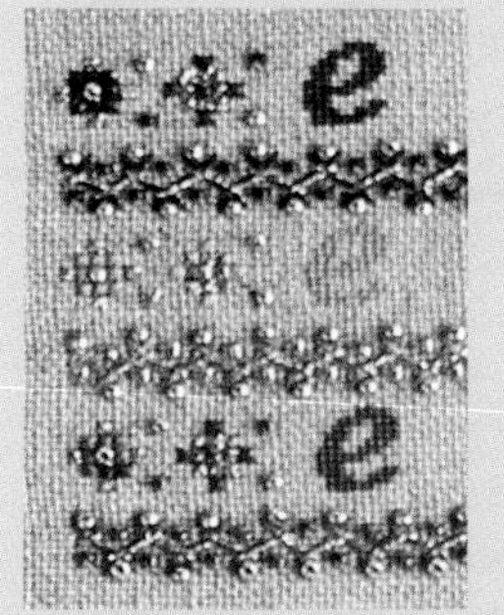

Experiment with other bead-and-thread color combinations to suit your decorating style. We've shown just a few possibilities *above.*

working with beads

When working with beads, it is important to get the bead to sit on its edge so the hole is not showing. There are two methods that work well to get this effect. The first is to stitch the bead with a half cross-stitch, using two plies of floss. Then come up to finish the cross-stitch and split the floss over the bead, pulling tightly.

The second method works better on softer fabrics (such as Cashel linen). Use one-ply floss and begin a cross-stitch. String the bead and complete the half cross-stitch. As you complete the cross-stitch, go through the hole again, pulling tightly.

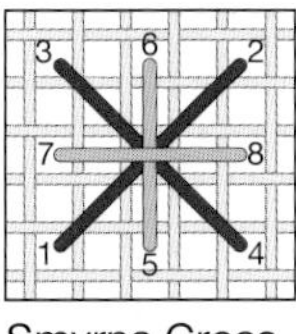

Smyrna Cross Variation

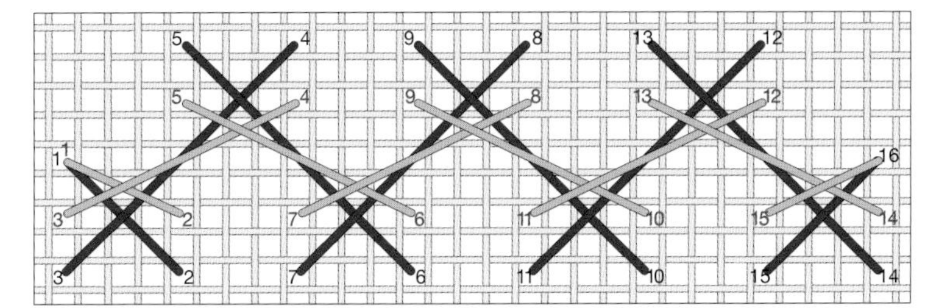

Layered Herringbone Stitch

Christmas Sampler Key

ANCHOR		DMC
CROSS-STITCH (2X)		
002	○	000 White
047	×	498 Christmas red
683	●	500 Blue-green
8581	^	646 Medium beaver gray
874	+	676 Old gold
1041	#	844 Deep beaver gray
022	★	902 Garnet
262	▲	3362 Loden

ANCHOR		DMC
BACKSTITCH (1X)		
1041	/	844 Deep beaver gray – all stitches
STRAIGHT STITCH (1X)		
1041	/	844 Deep beaver gray – jingle bells (1X); reindeer (2X)
FRENCH KNOT (1X wrapped twice)		
1041	•	844 Deep beaver gray – jingle bells

Stitch count: *159 high x 93 wide*

Finished design size:
14-count fabric – 11 3/8 x 6 2/3 inches

Christmas Sampler

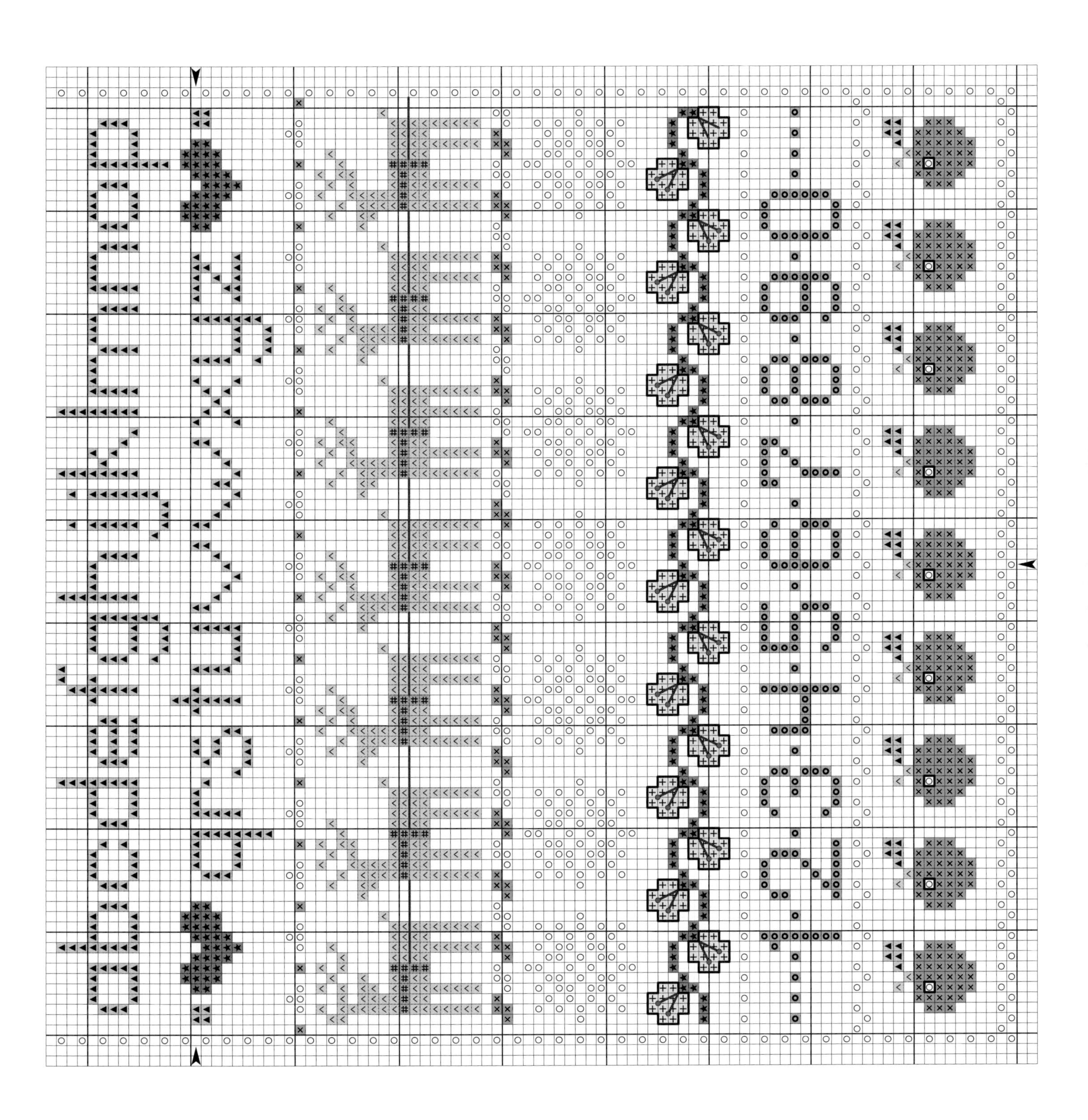

Poinsettia Box

Materials

28-count summer khaki Lugana fabric: 5×20" rectangle (lid sides); 8×20" rectangle (box sides)
Cotton embroidery floss
Purchased large canister set #1993
5"-diameter circle of fleece (lid top)
7"-diameter circle of red cotton fabric (lid top)
5"-diameter circle of felt (box bottom)
Delta Ceramcoat acrylic paint: Sandstone (2402)
Clear acrylic sealer
Sponge brush
Fusible webbing
Spray adhesive
Crafts glue

Instructions

For the lid sides, center and stitch the border motif from the Poinsettia Tray chart on *pages 46–47* on the 5×20" piece of Lugana fabric. Use three plies of floss to work the stitches over one square of the fabric unless otherwise specified.

For the box sides, center and baste a 16"-wide-by-3¼"-high rectangle on the remaining piece of Lugana fabric. Measure 5⅓" from the left side of the basted outline. Work a vertical line of basting there. Measure over another 5⅓" from that line of basting and insert another vertical line of basting. Center and stitch a poinsettia motif in the center of each basted shape.

Press the stitched pieces from the back. Centering the designs, trim the lid-side piece to measure 3×17" and the box-side piece to measure 4¾×17". Press the long edges of the box side piece under ¾". Set the pieces aside.

Assembly

Use a sponge brush to apply two coats of paint to the insides of the lid and box and both sides of the lid lip, allowing the paint to dry after each coat.

Use the spray adhesive to attach the fleece to the top of the lid. Trim the excess fleece close to the edge of the lid. Center the red fabric on the lid. Pull the fabric as taut as possible and smooth out any wrinkles. Press the raw edges over the sides of the lid and glue, clipping as necessary.

Press the lid side fabric lengthwise in thirds. The pressed lid piece should measure 1⅛" wide. Cut two strips of fusible webbing the same width and length as the lid piece. Slip one strip of fusible webbing underneath the long pressed edge and fuse, following the manufacturer's instructions. Press under the remaining long edge of the lid-side piece and fuse in the same manner. Press one short end of the lid-side piece under 1".

Apply glue to the back of the lid-side fabric. Beginning with the raw-edge end, stick the fabric to the lid's side, with the bottom edge of the fabric even with the edge of the lip of the lid, overlapping the folded short edge at the back.

Spread glue on the outer sides of the canister. Starting with the unfolded short edge of the rectangle, wrap the fabric around the canister, centering it on the sides of the canister. Overlap the folded edge to cover the raw edges at the back. Press down on the fabric to smooth out wrinkles and stick it to the canister. Glue the appropriate felt circle to each of the canister bottoms.

Poinsettia Tray

Materials

14×12" piece of 28-count summer khaki Lugana fabric
Cotton embroidery floss
Purchased 9×12" tray with a 7×10" design area (Sudberry #65658)
Fine-grit sandpaper
Clean cloth
Delta Ceramcoat acrylic paint: Sandstone (2402)
Sponge brush
9×12" piece of fleece
Spray adhesive
Thick white crafts glue or tape

Instructions

Center and stitch the Poinsettia Tray chart on *pages 46–47* on the Lugana fabric. Use three plies of floss to work the stitches over two threads of the fabric unless otherwise specified. Press the stitched piece from the back.

Remove the wood mat frame from the tray. Sand the unfinished side of the frame with fine-grit sandpaper. Remove the sanding dust with a clean cloth. Use a sponge brush to apply two coats of Sandstone paint to the unfinished side of the mat frame, allowing the paint to dry and sanding between coats.

Cut the fleece the same size as the mounting board from the tray. Spray the board lightly with the adhesive and position the fleece on top. Center the wrong side of the stitched piece over the fleece on the board; tape or glue the edges to the back. Insert the painted mat frame and the design into the tray; reassemble the tray following the manufacturer's instructions.

Holly Pillow

Materials

13" square of 14-count black Aida cloth
Cotton embroidery floss
1/3 yard of red cotton fabric
1/3 yard of red metallic fabric
1 yard of 1/2"-diameter cording
Matching sewing thread
Polyester fiberfill

Instructions

Center and stitch the Holly Pillow chart on *pages 48–49* on the Aida cloth. Use three plies of floss to work the stitches over one square of the fabric unless otherwise specified. Press the stitched piece from the back.

Centering the design, trim the stitched piece into an 8" square. From the red cotton fabric, cut one 11½" square for the back and four 2¾×11½" strips for the flange. From the red metallic fabric, cut enough 2"-wide bias strips to make a 36" length of piping. When sewing the pieces together, use a ½" seam allowance with right sides facing unless otherwise specified.

Sew the short ends of the 2"-wide bias strips together to make a continuous length. Center the cording lengthwise on the wrong side of the piping strip. Fold the fabric around the cording, long edges even. Use a zipper foot to sew through both layers, close to the cording.

With raw edges even, use a zipper foot to baste the piping around the perimeter of the trimmed stitched piece, clipping the piping at the corners to lay flat.

Use a zipper foot to sew a flange strip to each edge of stitched piece along the basting line, starting and stopping 1" from the edges of the stitched piece. Pin and sew to miter the corners of the flange strips. Trim excess flange fabric; press open the mitered seams. Press the remaining seams toward the flange.

Sew the assembled pillow front to the back, leaving a 3" opening along one edge for turning. Trim the seams and clip the corners. Turn the pillow right side out; press. Pin the front to the back as close as possible to the inner edge of the flange. Use a zipper foot to sew through all layers close to the inner edge of the flange next to the piping, leaving an opening to correspond to the first opening.

Stuff the pillow firmly. Using a zipper foot, sew the opening closed at the inner edge of the flange; slip-stitch the outer opening closed.

Poinsettia Tray Key

ANCHOR		DMC
CROSS-STITCH (3X)		
019	☆	304 Medium Christmas red
013	=	321 True Christmas red
255	▽	470 Medium avocado
265	+	471 Light avocado
254	/	472 Pale avocado
045	♥	814 Dark garnet
044	×	815 Medium garnet
1005	○	816 Light garnet
817	●	3345 Medium hunter green
267	□	3346 True hunter green
266	I	3347 Light hunter green
306	*	3820 Straw
BACKSTITCH (1X)		
268	/	469 Dark avocado
246	/	986 Forest green

Stitch count: *83 high x 119 wide*

Finished design size:
28-count fabric – 6 x 8½ inches

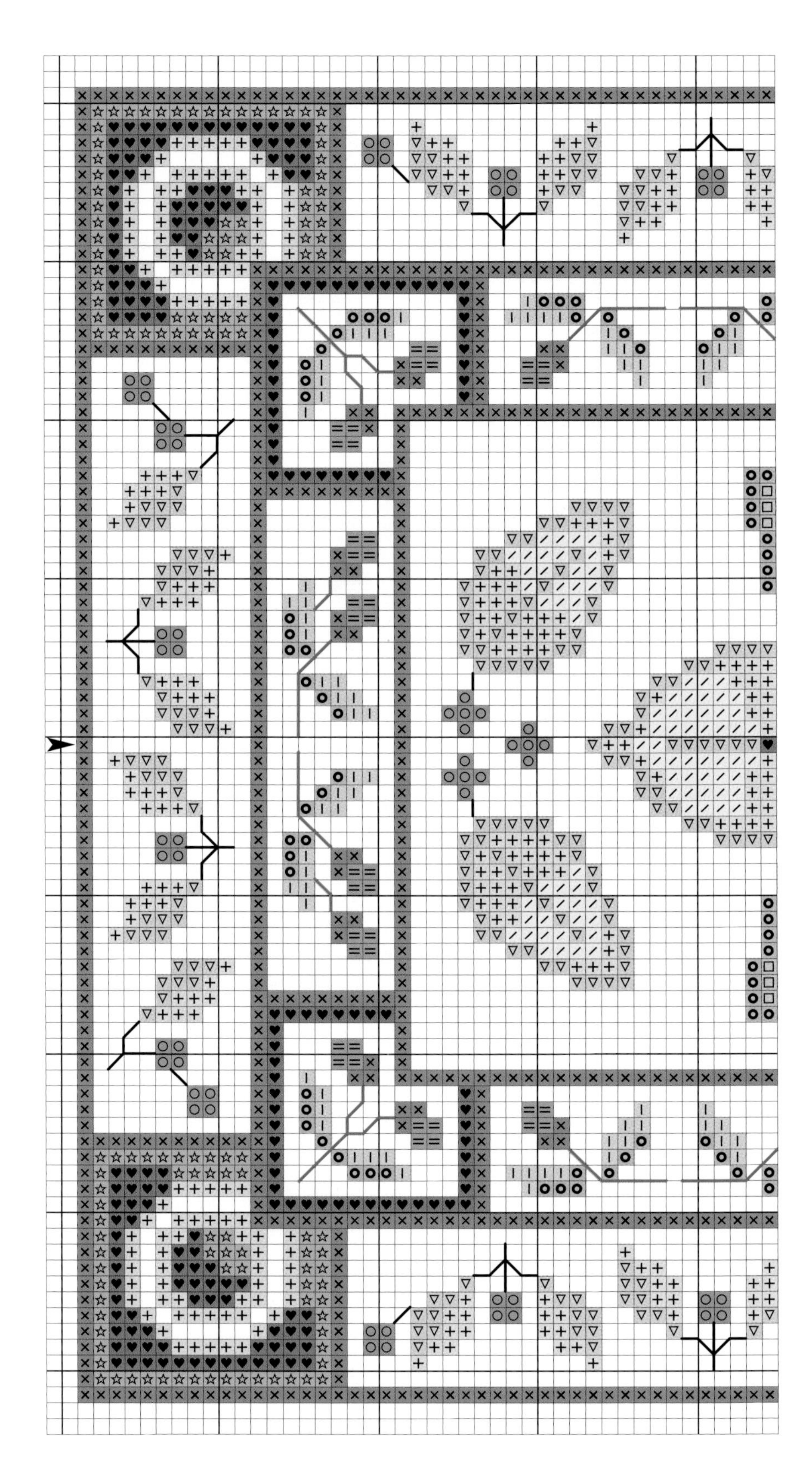

The Legend of the Poinsettia

Poinsettias are native to Mexico, where they grow wild. The legend of the poinsettia grew from a tale that dates back several hundred years to a Christmas Eve in Mexico. A little girl named Pepita, the story says, had no gift to bring to the Christ Child. Her cousin Pedro told her that a gift from the heart, no matter how humble, would please the Child. On her way to church, she gathered some weeds she found along the road. As she approached the altar, a miracle happened: The weeds blossomed into brilliant flowers. They were called Flores de Noche Buena—Flowers of the Holy Night. Today we call those flowers poinsettias.

They are named after Joel Robert Poinsett, who was an amateur botanist and the first ambassador to Mexico. In 1825 Poinsett brought some cuttings to his plantation in South Carolina. Poinsett died in 1851. To honor him and the plant he introduced to the United States, December 12—the date of his death—was established as National Poinsettia Day.

Deck the Halls

Deck the Halls

Holly Pillow Key

ANCHOR		DMC
CROSS-STITCH (3X)		
013	⊠	321 True Christmas red
267	⊞	469 Dark avocado
266	▽	470 Medium avocado
265	^	471 Light avocado
254	−	472 Pale avocado
047	◆	498 Dark Christmas red
246	▲	986 Forest green
817	#	3345 Medium hunter green
267	*	3346 True hunter green
266	○	3347 Light hunter green
035	I	3705 Watermelon
001	•	B5200 Bright white

Stitch count: *94 high x 94 wide*

Finished design size:
14-count fabric – 6¾ x 6¾ inches

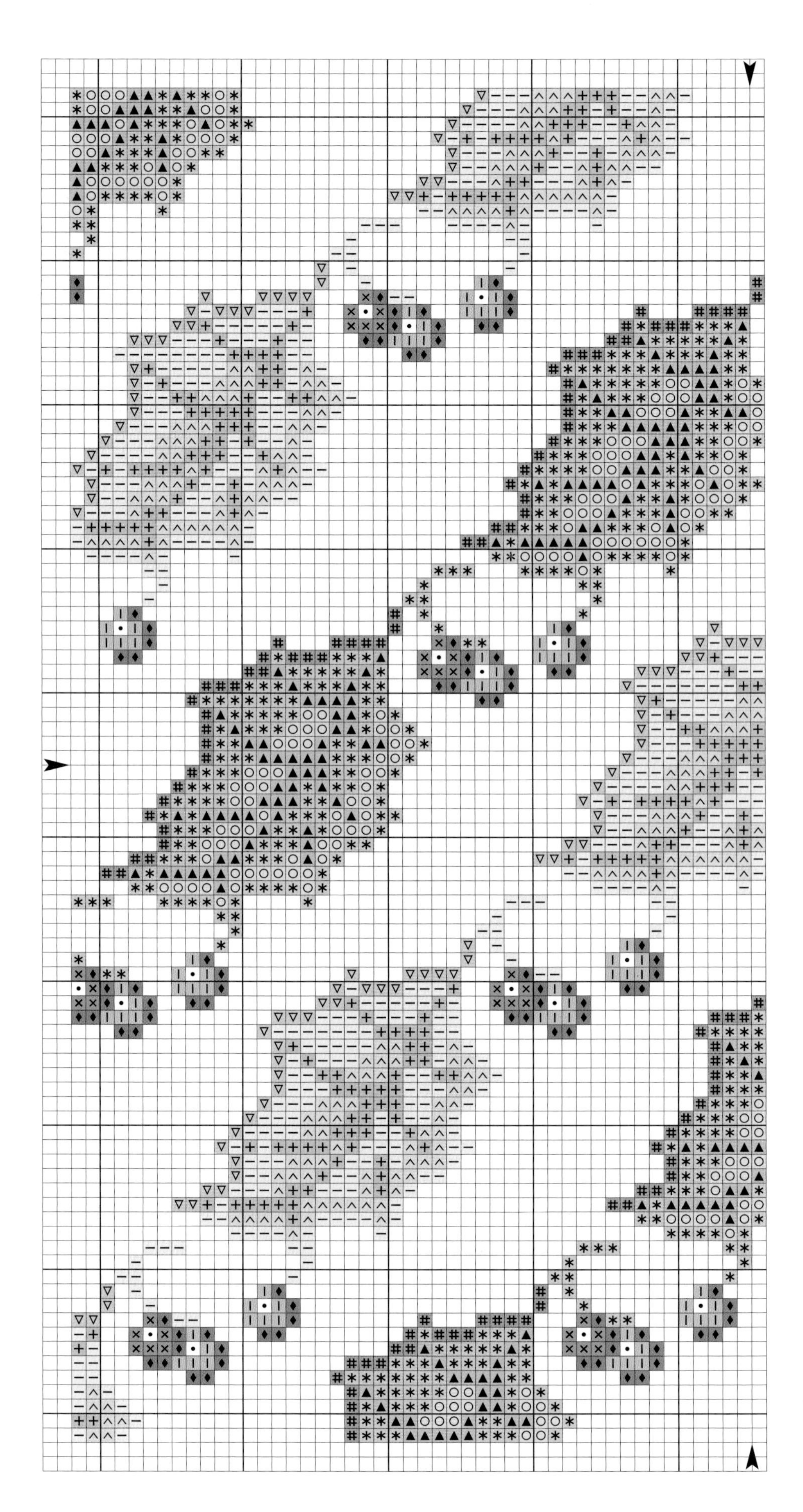

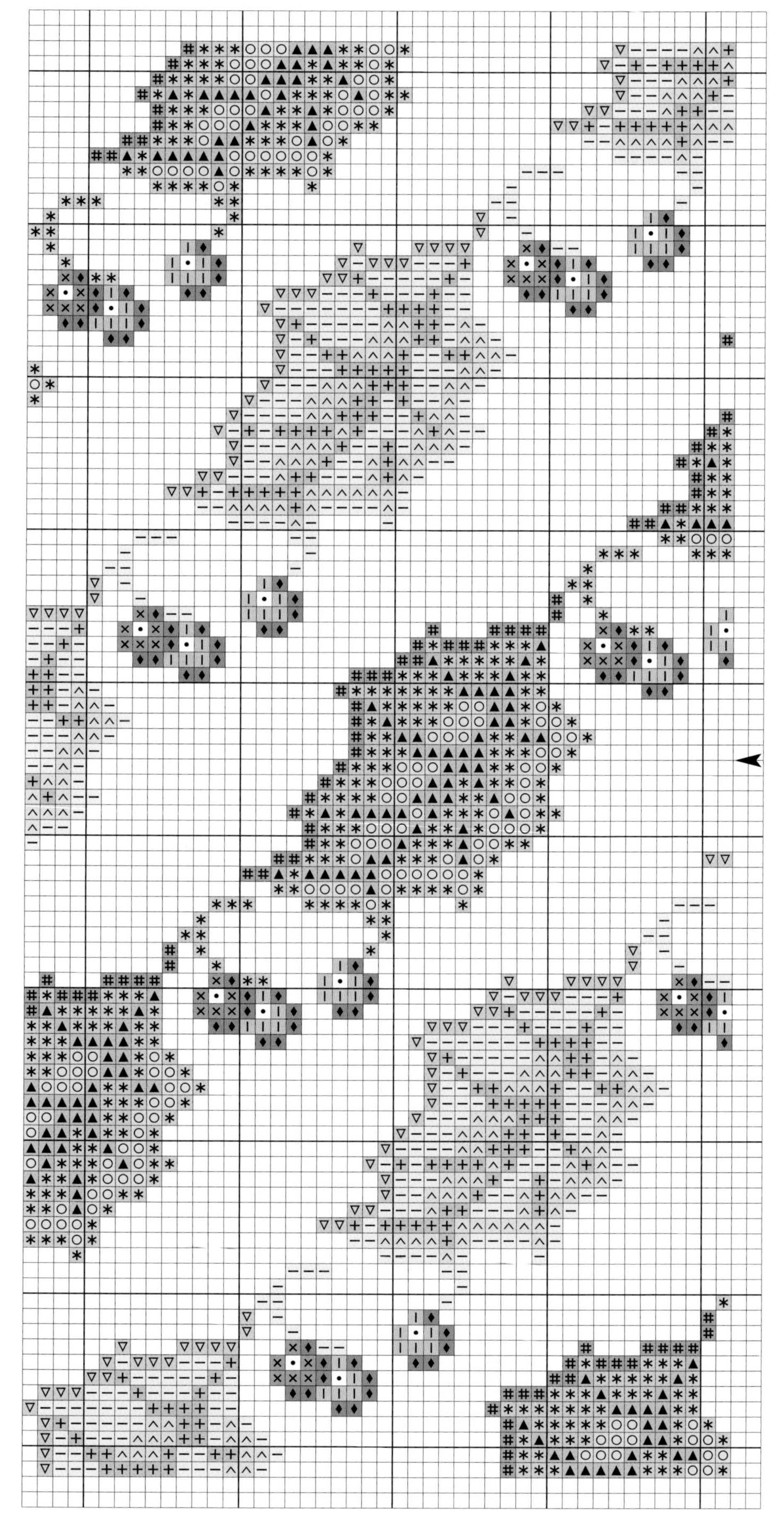

Holly and Ivy

The holly tree's combination of glossy green leaves and brilliant red berries makes it a natural for holiday decorating. But long before it was popular for its red-and-white color scheme, holly was revered for its supposed magical powers.

From early times, primitive tribes hung holly above doorways to entice woodland spirits into their homes during that darkest time of the year, winter solstice. Later, a Christmas tradition grew that holly had sprung from Jesus' footsteps as he walked the earth preaching the gospel. It was used in churches at Christmastime and called the holy tree.

Holly and ivy are spoken of together in the English Christmas carol "The Holly and the Ivy." They also share the same red-and-green color scheme, as the kind of ivy grown in England turns red in the fall.

It was believed that "whosoever brings holly into the house first, either husband or wife, shall rule the home during the coming year." Although the English church frowned upon ivy as pagan—it was associated in Greek times with fruitfulness and with the god of wine, Dionysius—it was still widely used as decoration, as reflected in this 16th-century verse:

So now is come our joyfulst feast,
Let each man be jolly.
Each room with ivy leaves is dressed,
And every post with holly.

Ornament Box Tray

Materials

13×15" piece of 28-count ivory Lugana fabric
Cotton embroidery floss
Kreinik #4 very fine braid
Kreinik blending filament
Purchased 9×12" petite oak tray with a 7×10" design area (Sudberry #65008)

Instructions

Center and stitch the Ornament Box Tray chart on *pages 52–53* on the fabric. Use three plies of floss or one strand of braid to work the cross-stitches over two threads of the fabric. Work the remaining stitches as specified in the key. Press the finished piece carefully from the back. Insert the stitched piece into the tray following manufacturer's instructions.

Quick and Easy Ornaments

Materials

For each ornament:
3" square of 14-count white perforated plastic or 14-count white perforated paper
Cotton embroidery floss
Kreinik #4 very fine braid
Kreinik blending filament
3" square of white felt
Crafts glue

Instructions

Center and stitch the desired ornament from the Ornament Box tray chart on *pages 52–53* on the perforated plastic or the perforated paper.

Use three plies of floss or one strand of braid to work the cross-stitches over one square of perforated plastic or perforated paper. Work the blended-needle stitches and other stitches as specified.

When stitching is complete, use one strand of Gold filament (Kreinik 202HL) to backstitch the ornament loop. For the blue ornament with the gold center, use two plies of Dark cornflower blue floss (DMC 791) to work long straight stitches.

When all stitching is complete, cut out each ornament shape one square beyond the stitching, being careful not to cut into a hole that contains a stitch. Use the stitched shape to cut a matching back from the felt.

For hanging loop, thread a needle with gold braid. Thread the braid through the center top of the ornament; knot ends. Glue the felt to the back of the ornament.

TIP
finish ornaments like a pro

The relatively small size of most ornaments makes them popular stitching projects. To finish ornaments with flair, try one of these easy ideas.

A perforated plastic ornament, *far right,* is simple to finish. Trim around the stitching and add a hanger of floss or metallic thread, or mount it on felt or suede cloth.

A simple fabric ornament, *right,* also can be fringed and mounted on felt or suede cloth. To prevent the fringe from raveling, machine-sew around the edges.

Or finish a small stitched piece as a miniature pillow, *right.* Assemble following the directions for the Noel Ornament on *page 76.*

Quilt sashing enhances the country look of simple pieces. Decide the width of the sashing strips and add ¼" seam allowances. Sew strips to the top and bottom. If you like cornerstones (corner squares), cut them the width of the strips and sew to the side strip ends before attaching the strips to the center.

Another easy finish for cross-stitch ornaments is self-stick mounting board. It's available with or without foam that gives your piece a nice padded look. You'll find several ornament-ready sizes and shapes. It's also available in 5×7" and 8×10" sheets. These are designed to accommodate framed pieces, but they can be cut into smaller sizes and shapes with a crafts knife. Most are made from archival-quality materials that won't damage your fabric or stitching. Follow the manufacturer's directions and add a piece of felt cut to shape for a neat back side.

Crafts and stitching stores also sell a variety of simple mounting kits—no sewing required—in many shapes and sizes.

Perforated plastic ornament

Fabric ornament finished as a pillow with fringed edges

Ornament on a mounting board

Ornament Box

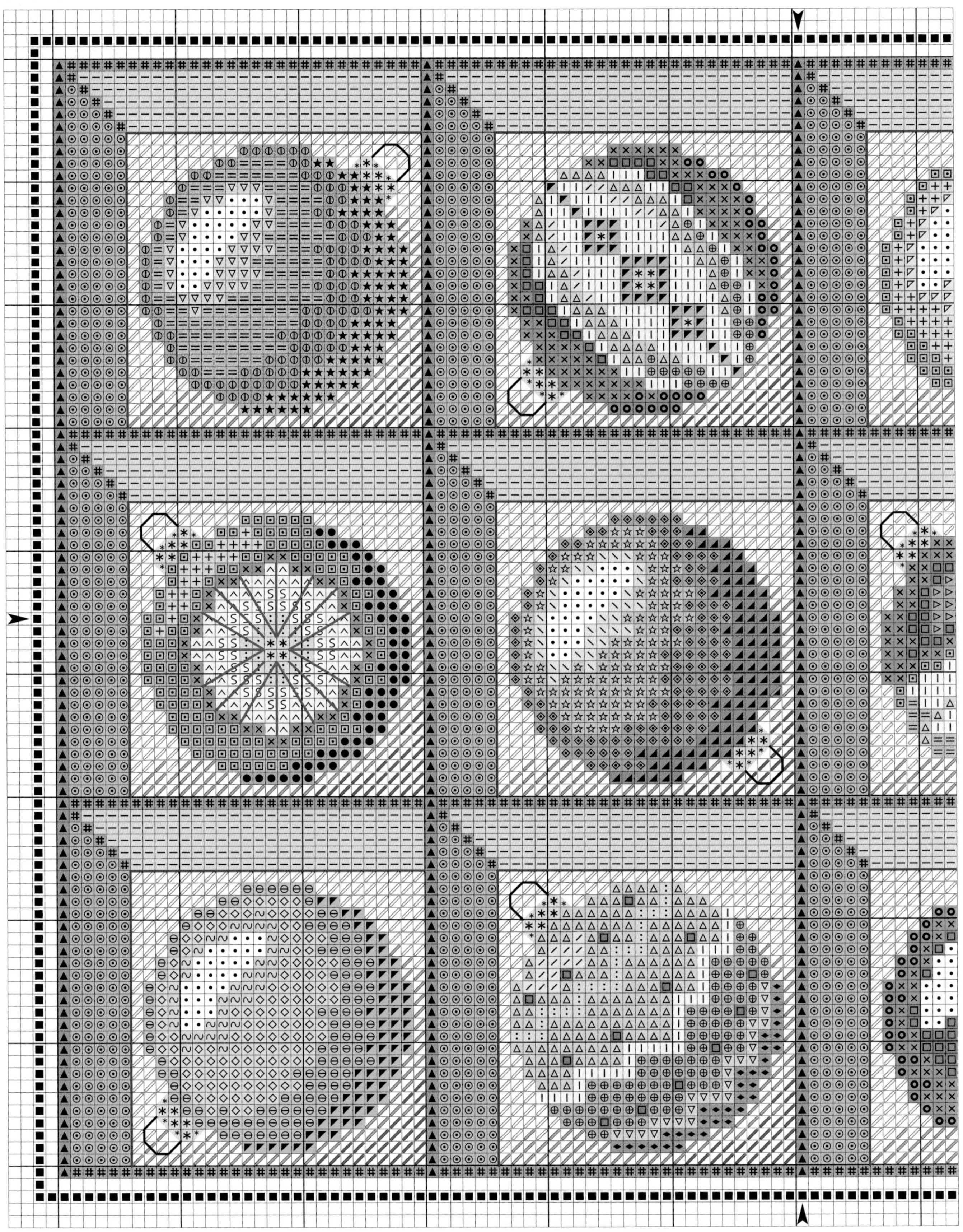

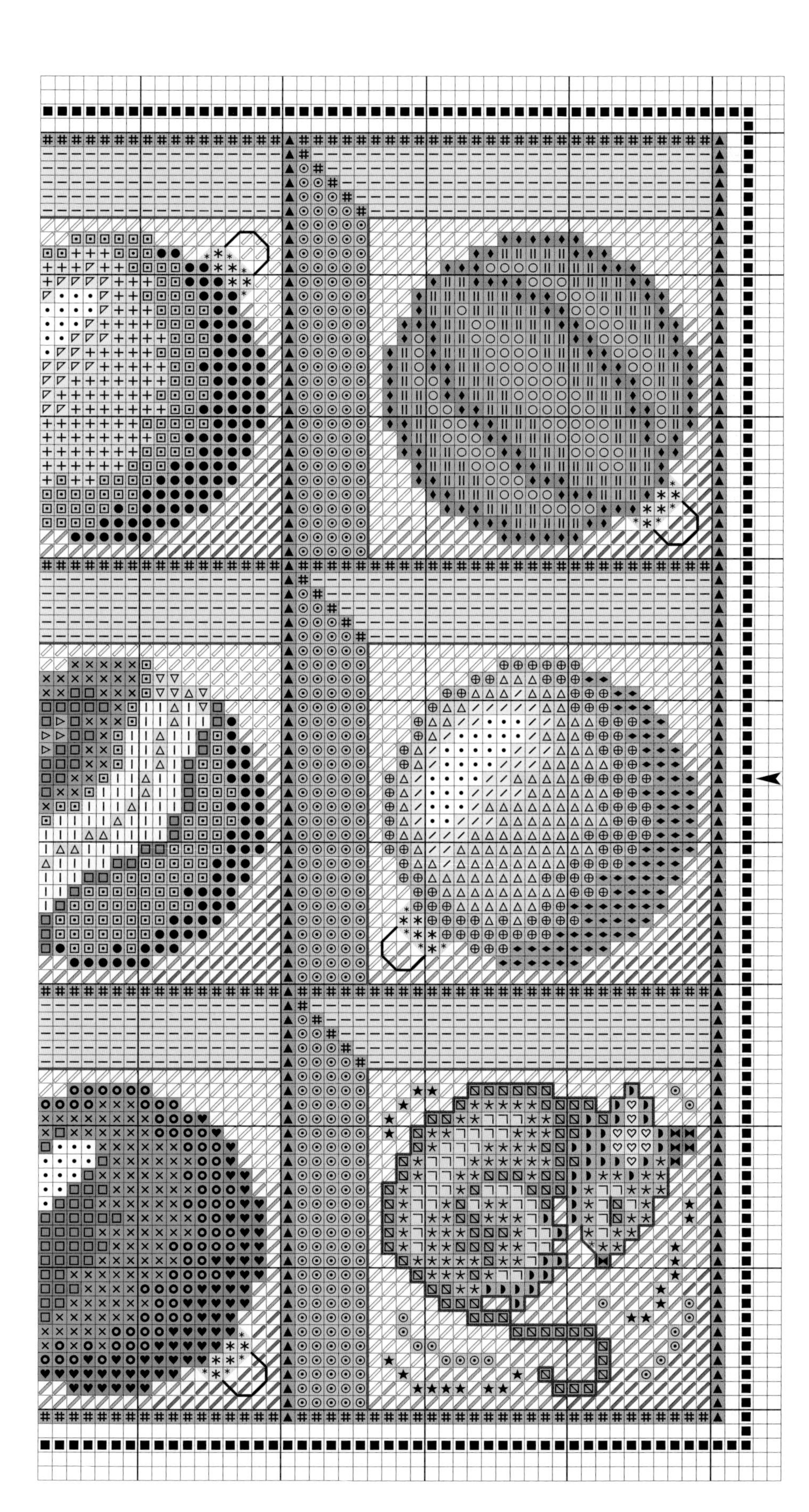

ANCHOR		DMC
CROSS-STITCH (2X)		
892	♡	225 Shell pink
019	♥	304 Medium Christmas red
013	◘	321 True Christmas red
371	#	433 Dark caramel
1046	⊙	435 True caramel
362	–	437 Pale caramel
102	◢	550 Deep violet
101	◈	552 Dark violet
099	☆	553 Medium violet
098	╲	554 Light violet
046	×	666 Red
088	‖	718 True plum
301	^	744 Medium yellow
300	S	745 Light yellow
307	★	783 True Christmas gold
178	●	791 Deep cornflower blue
177	▣	792 Medium cornflower blue
176	+	793 True cornflower blue
175	◸	794 Light cornflower blue
358	▲	801 True coffee brown
169	⊖	806 Dark peacock blue
168	◇	807 Medium peacock blue
359	■	898 Dark coffee brown
229	◆	909 Dark emerald
228	⊕	910 True emerald
227	△	911 Medium emerald
205	⁄	912 Light emerald
065	◆	915 Deep plum
905	⧓	3021 Deep brown-gray
392	⊠	3022 Medium brown-gray
1040	★	3023 Light brown-gray
397	⌐	3024 Pale brown-gray
292	I	3078 Topaz
086	○	3608 Light plum
031	▷	3706 Pale watermelon
170	◤	3765 Deep peacock blue
167	∾	3766 Light peacock blue
273	◗	3787 Dark brown-gray
1098	▢	3801 True watermelon
306	⦶	3820 Dark straw
305	=	3821 True straw
891	▽	3822 Light straw
386	⁚	3823 Pale yellow
	✱	202HL Kreinik gold #4 Hi-Lustre very fine braid
BLENDED-NEEDLE CROSS-STITCH		
926	•	Ecru (2X) and 032 Kreinik pearl blending filament (1X)
HALF CROSS-STITCH (1X)		
590	╱	712 Cream
361	╱	738 Light tan
942	╱	739 Pale tan
BACKSTITCH (1X)		
371	╱	433 Dark caramel – inner box lines
905	╱	3021 Deep brown-gray – ornament loops (2X); mouse eyelid (1X)
273	╱	3787 Dark brown-gray – mouse body (1X)
STRAIGHT STITCH		
178	╱	791 Deep cornflower blue – detail of left orament in row two

Stitch count: *95 high x 125 wide*

Finished design size:
28-count fabric – 6¾ x 9 inches

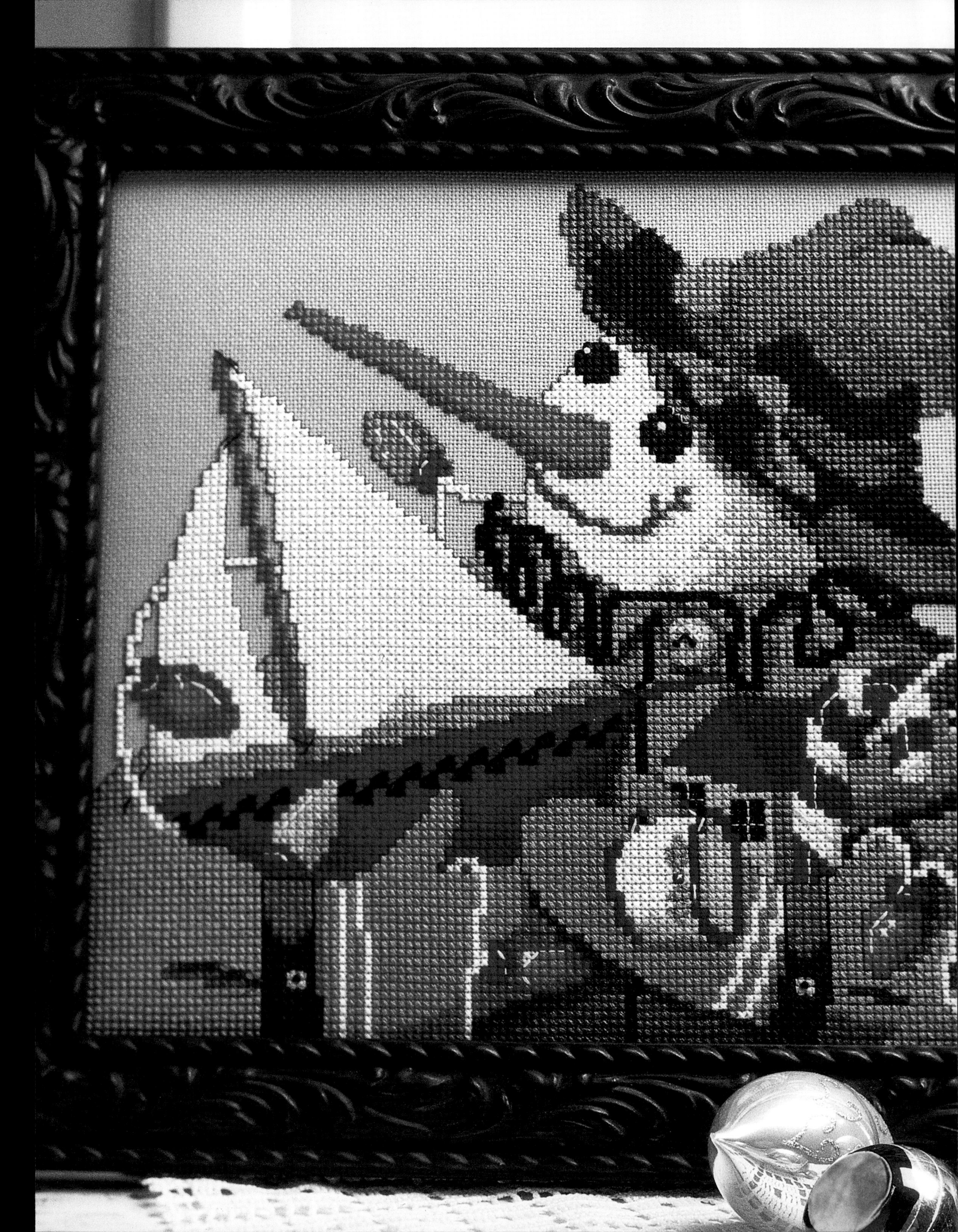

Snowman celebration

If you fancy snowmen or know a snowman collector, you'll love this grouping of cheery designs. These frosty fellows won't melt away on a sunny day or if you leave them in a warm room. Stitch one or all of the designs. Then place them around your home or share them with a friend, and hearts will melt away.

Project instructions begin on page 62.
Design: watercolor by Kathy Schmitz, cross-stitch translation by Barbara Sestok
Photography: Hopkins Associates

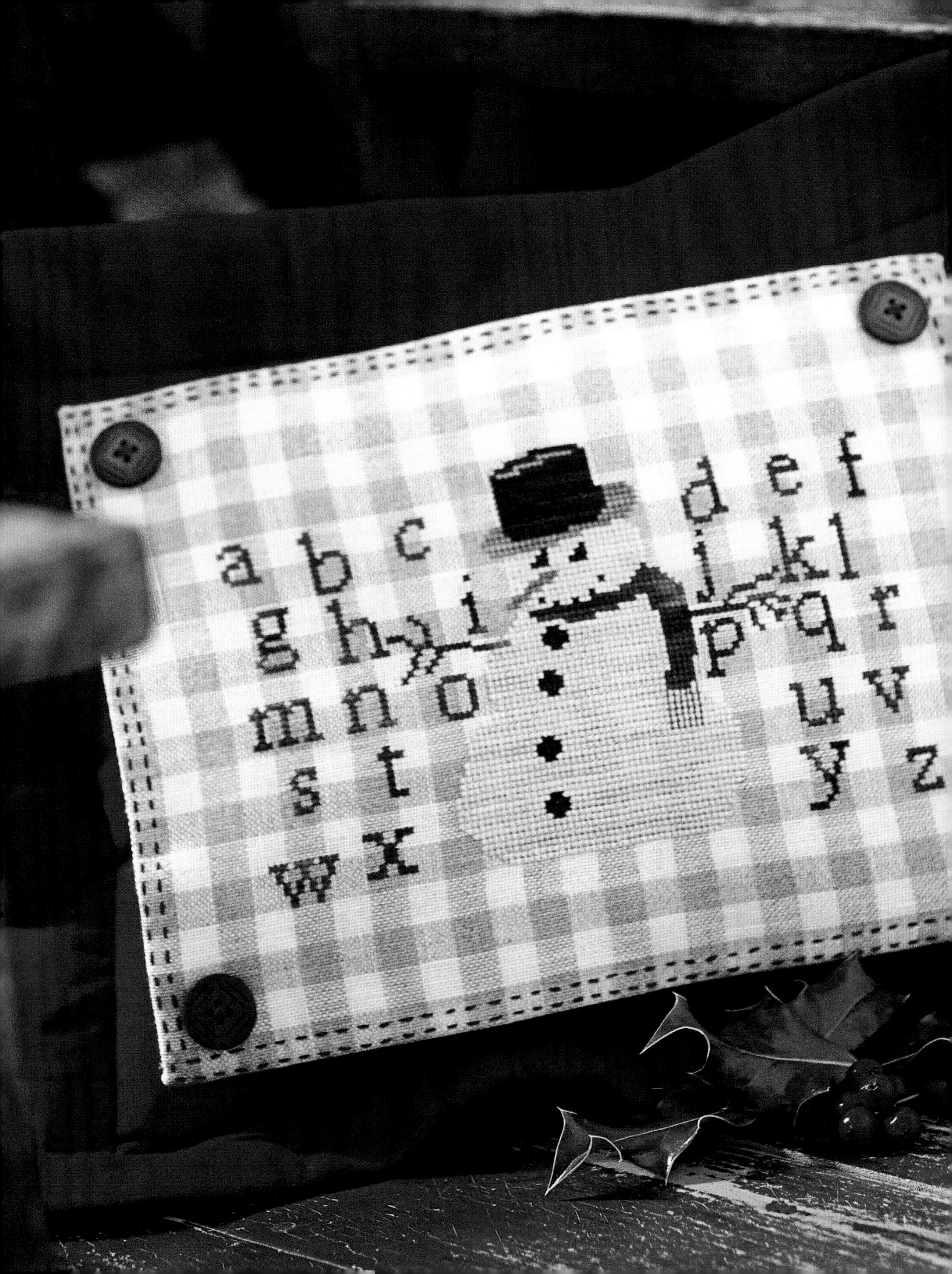

a b c d e f
g h i j k l
m n o p q r
s t u v
w x y z

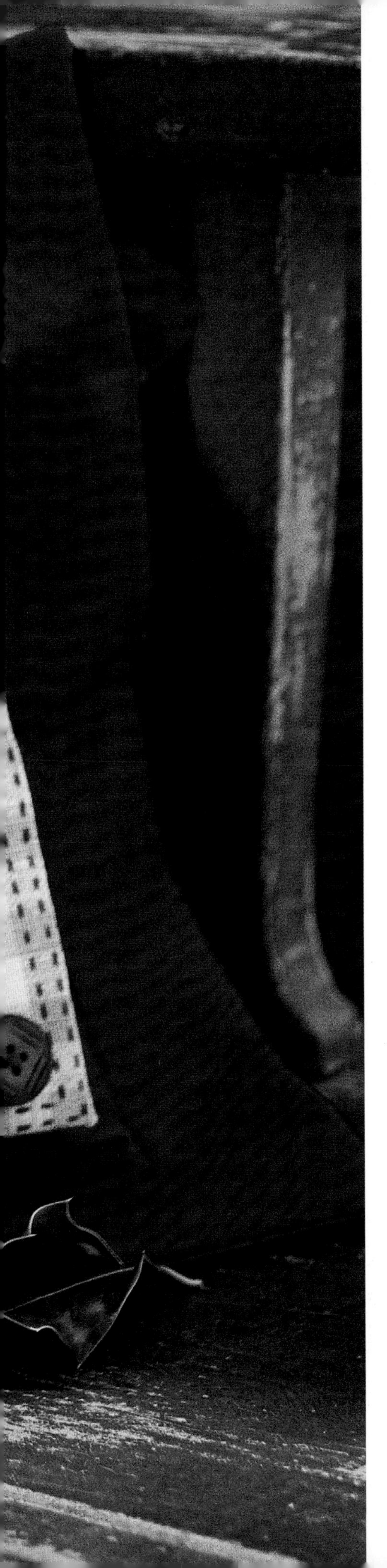

Snowman
celebration

Perky gingham fabric makes our country snowman the star of the delightful pillow at *left*. We've included complete finishing instructions for this fun-to-stitch design, but you also could button the piece onto a purchased pillow. And what a difference stitching over a single thread can make! Work the snowman over one thread of fabric; then frame it with a printed fabric border to create a fabulous ornament, *above*.

Project instructions begin on page 64.

Design: Ruth Sparrow Gendron • Photography: Hopkins Associates

White cross-stitches bring the snowman and snow woman on these darling stockings *above* to life. This whimsical couple is loaded with personality, and the stockings are the perfect size to hold treats of all kinds or tiny gifts.

Project instructions begin on page 66.

Design: Laura Holtorf Collins • Photography: Hopkins Associates

This joyous fellow *opposite* is celebrating winter with his arms outstretched, catching every snowflake that falls nearby. He's dressed for the part, too, with a warm scarf, snug cap, and fluffy earmuffs. The beaded and backstitched border treatment frames the design perfectly.

Project instructions begin on page 69.

Design: Denise Zakalik • Photography: Scott Little

LET IT SNOW!

This tiny treasure left is a marvel to behold. Your family and friends will be enthralled by the dainty silk stitches worked over one thread of silk gauze to create this miniature marvel.

Project instructions begin on page 69.

Design: Kreinik • Photography: Hopkins Associates

The same snowman design worked in big stitches results in big impact as seen in the pillow *opposite*. The result is a rustic, informal look, plus the Klostern fabric means that counting is easy on the eyes.

Project instructions begin on page 69.

Design: Kreinik • Photography: Dean Tanner

Snowman
celebration

Snowman with Toys

This charming watercolor created by artist Kathy Schmitz, was the inspiration for the cross-stitch piece shown on page 54.

Snowman with Toys

Materials

16×18" piece of 25-count wedgwood Lugana Fabric
Cotton embroidery floss
Desired frame

Instructions

Center and stitch the Snowman with Toys chart at *right* on the fabric. Use three plies of floss to work the stitches over two threads of the fabric unless otherwise specified. Press the stitched piece from the back. Frame as desired.

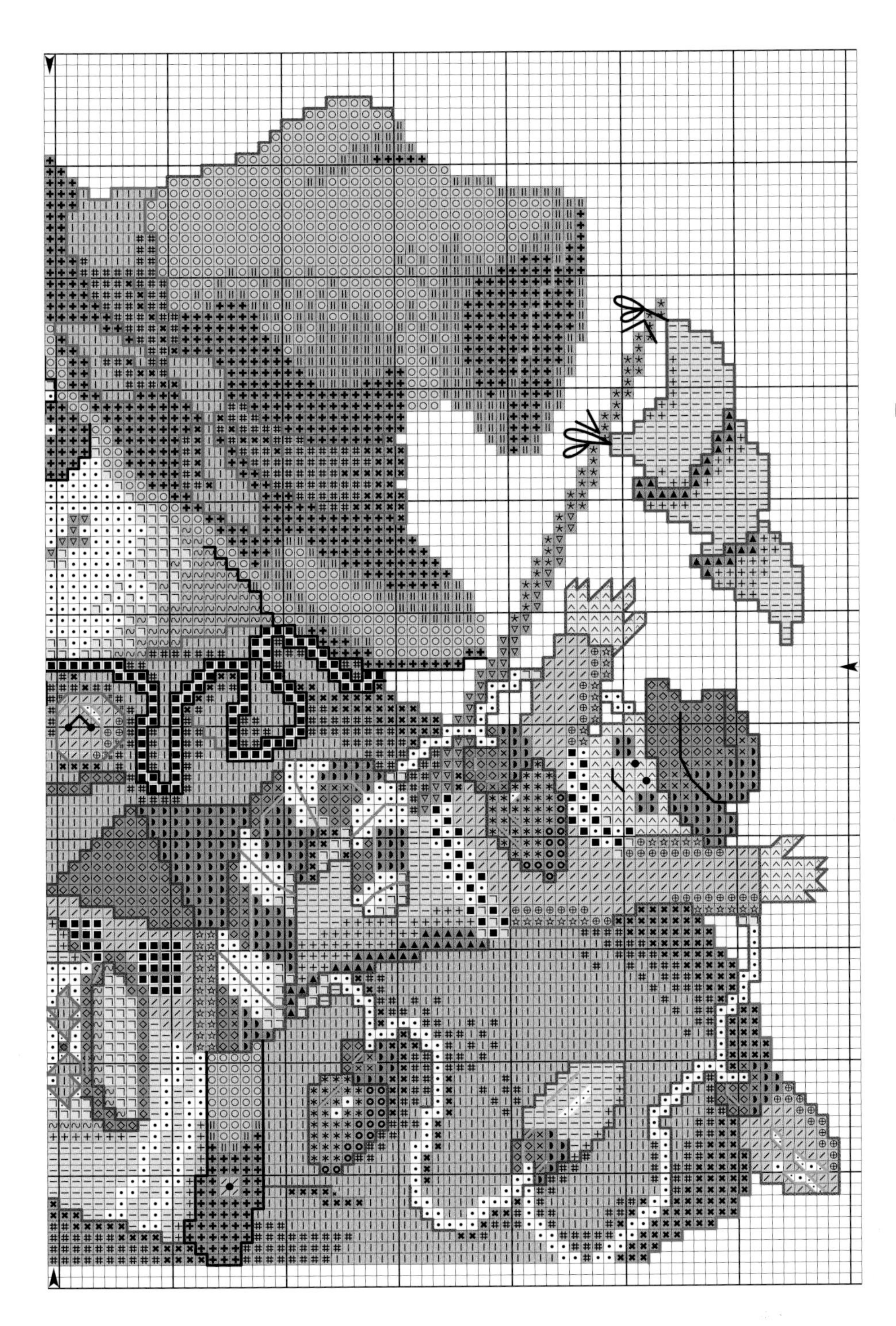

Snowman with Toys Key

ANCHOR DMC

CROSS-STITCH (3X)

- 002 • 000 White
- 150 ▲ 336 Navy
- 370 ☆ 434 Caramel
- 047 ◇ 817 Coral
- 862 ✖ 934 Pine green
- 332 ✱ 946 Burnt orange
- 006 ^ 967 Melon
- 355 ▽ 975 Deep golden brown
- 1001 ⊕ 976 Medium golden brown
- 263 # 3051 Dark gray-green
- 860 | 3052 Medium gray-green
- 1007 ★ 3772 Cocoa
- 1015 ◗ 3777 Terra-cotta
- 122 + 3807 Dark blue-violet
- 176 — 3839 Medium blue-violet
- 313 / 3854 Autumn gold

BLENDED NEEDLE CROSS-STITCH

- 072 / 382 ✚ 154 Deep grape (1X) and 3371 Black-brown (2X)
- 343 / 939 ∾ 159 Light blue-gray (2X) and 160 Medium blue-gray (1X)
- 403 / 382 ■ 310 Black (2X) and 3371 Black-brown (1X)
- 398 / 120 ⌐ 415 Light pearl gray (1X) and 3747 Pale periwinkle (2X)
- 1086 / 872 ‖ 779 Dark plum-brown (1X) and 3740 Dark antique violet (2X)
- 047 / 1015 ✕ 817 Coral (2X) and 3777 Terra-cotta (1X)
- 339 / 332 ◉ 920 Copper (2X) and 946 Burnt orange (1X)
- 871 / 354 ○ 3041 Medium antique violet (2X) and 3860 Medium plum-brown (1X)

BACKSTITCH

- 002 / 000 White – hat detail, lights, button, candy cane (1X)
- 403 / 310 Black – hat (1X)
- 150 / 336 Navy – doll, flag, mittens (1X)
- 370 / 434 Caramel – doll skirt, gold lighthouse (2X); doll hands (1X)
- 1041 / 844 Deep beaver gray – lights, snowman face, hat, collar, boat, mittens, candy cane (1X)
- 339 / 920 Copper – carrot (2X)
- 862 / 934 Pine green – hat detail, cup leaves
- 1015 / 3777 Terra-cotta – boat, lights, cup, hat (2X); doll hat detail (3X)
- 313 / 3854 Autumn gold – cuff button, candy cane, windows

BLENDED BACKSTITCH

- 403 / 382 / 310 Black (1X) and 3371 Black-brown (1X) – hat, collar, cuffs, boat

STRAIGHT STITCH

- 002 / 000 White – berry cup

FRENCH KNOT (1X wrapped twice)

- 002 ● 000 White – snowman eyes
- 403 ● 310 Black – buttons, doll eyes

LAZY DAISY

- 403 0 310 Black – ties on flag

Stitch count: *104 high x 139 wide*

Finished design size:
25-count fabric – 8 1/3 x 11 1/8 inches

Snowman celebration

Gingham Snowman Pillow

Materials

- 14×11" piece of 28-count natural/cream Riviera gingham fabric
- Sampler Threads overdyed floss
- ½ yard of red cotton fabric
- 17½×15" rectangle of medium-weight quilt batting
- Matching sewing thread
- Polyester fiberfill
- 10½×8" piece of fusible fleece
- Red cotton embroidery floss
- Four ¾"-diameter red buttons

Instructions

Center and stitch the Gingham Snowman chart *opposite* on the fabric. Use three plies of floss to work the stitches over two threads of the fabric unless otherwise specified. When working with overdyed floss, complete each cross-stitch before beginning the next. Press the stitched piece from the back.

From the red fabric, cut two 17½×15" rectangles. Place the quilt batting on a flat surface. Center and smooth one red rectangle, right side up, on the batting. Center and smooth the second red rectangle, right side down, on the first. Pin-baste all layers together. Sew the layers together ½" from the edges, leaving an opening along one long edge for turning. Trim the batting close to the stitching. Trim the seams and clip the corners. Turn the pillow right side out and press. To create the flange, sew 2" from the edges of the pillow, leaving an opening to correspond with the first opening. Firmly stuff the pillow with polyester fiberfill between the batting and the pillow back. Using a zipper foot, sew the opening closed at the inner edge of the flange. Slip-stitch the outer opening closed.

Centering the design, trim the stitched piece to measure 13×10½". Center and fuse the fleece to the back. Press the unfused edges to the back, mitering the corners. Use three plies of red floss to sew running stitches close to the edges of the stitched piece and then again ⅛" inside the first lines of stitches. Sew a button to each corner of the stitched piece. Center the stitched piece on the pillow front, and tack the corners to the pillow fabric.

Country Snowman Ornament

Materials

- 8" square of 28-count Christmas red Jubilee fabric
- Sampler Threads overdyed floss
- ¼ yard of red-print cotton fabric
- Scrap of green-print cotton fabric
- Matching sewing thread
- Polyester fiberfill
- Seven ½"-diameter buttons
- Fine twine
- 24" length of 18-gauge copper wire
- Pencil

Instructions

Center and stitch the snowman motif from the Gingham Snowman Pillow chart *opposite* on the fabric. Use one ply of floss to work the stitches over one thread of fabric unless otherwise specified. When working with overdyed floss, complete each cross-stitch before beginning the next. Press the stitched piece from the back.

Centering the design, trim the piece into a 4" square. Cut four 1¼×4" sashing strips and one 5½" square ornament back from the red-print fabric. Cut four 1¼" squares from the green-print fabric. Measurements include ¼" seam allowances.

Sew a sashing strip to the left and right edges of the stitched piece; press the seams toward the strips. Sew a 1¼" green-print square to each end of the remaining sashing strips; press the seams toward the strips. Sew one pieced strip to the top of the stitched piece and one to the bottom, matching the seams, to complete the ornament front. Press seams toward the sashing strips.

Sew the ornament front to the back, leaving an opening at the bottom of the piece for turning; trim corners. Turn the ornament right side out and press. Lightly stuff the ornament with polyester fiberfill. Slip-stitch the opening closed. Use twine to attach a button to each corner of the ornament, knotting the twine on the front of buttons.

For the hanger, wrap the wire around a pencil to coil. Remove the pencil and shape the wire into a hanger. Slip the remaining buttons onto the wire, spacing as desired. Wrap the wire around the top corner buttons of the ornament about 2" from the end to create the coiled ends.

Gingham Snowman Pillow Key

ANCHOR	DMC	SAMPLER THREAD
CROSS-STITCH (3X)		
403 ■	310 Black	1040 Black crow
370 ▲	434 Caramel	510 Cinnamon
323 ⊕	722 Bittersweet	560 Nutmeg

ANCHOR	DMC	SAMPLER THREAD
CROSS-STITCH (3X)		
246 ⊠	986 Forest green	190 Forest glade
236 ☰	3799 Charcoal	1140 Oatmeal
002 ⊡	3865 Winter white	1030 Banker's gray

ANCHOR	DMC	SAMPLER THREAD
BACKSTITCH (1X)		
246 /	986 Forest green – scarf fringe	190 Forest glade

Stitch count: *66 high x 108 wide*

Finished design size:
28-count fabric – $4\frac{3}{4}$ x $7\frac{2}{3}$ inches

Gingham Snowman Pillow

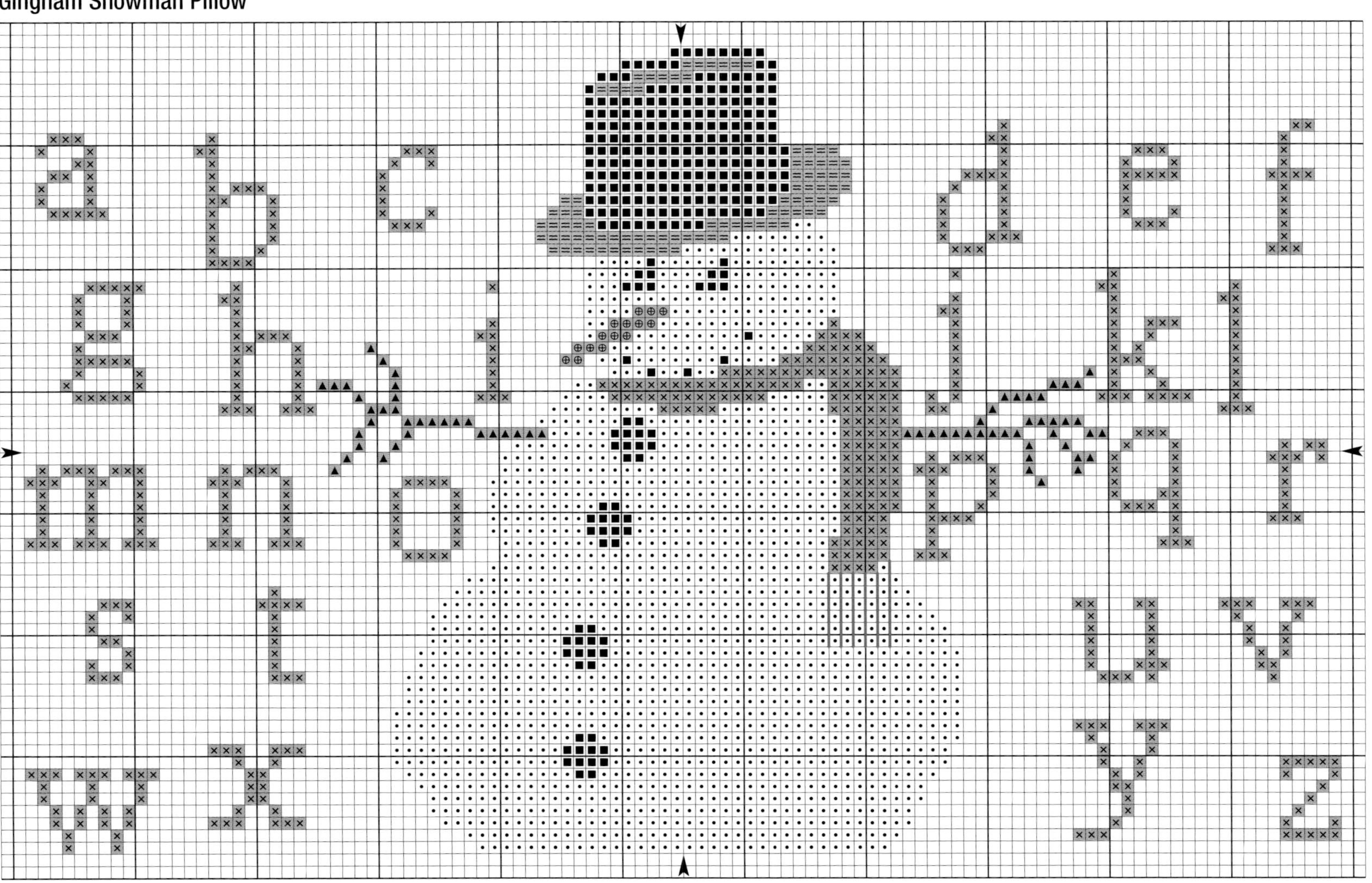

Snowman
celebration

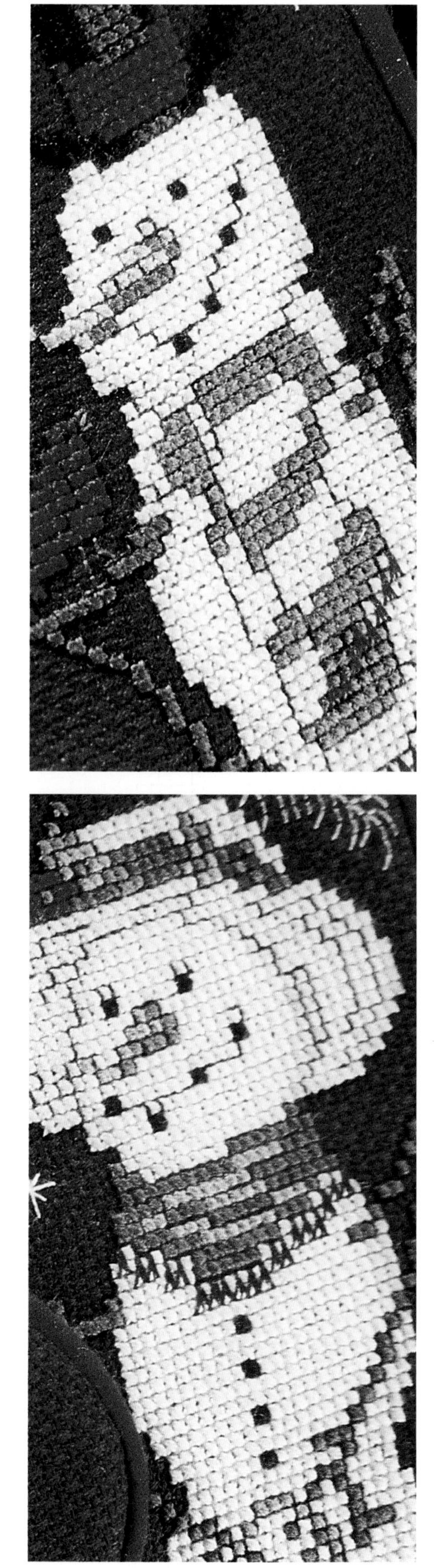

Snowman and Snow Woman Stockings

Materials

For each stocking:

10×14" piece of 14-count navy Aida cloth
Cotton embroidery floss
Erasable fabric marker
10×12" piece of fusible fleece
1⁄3 yard of red cotton fabric
1 yard of narrow cording
Matching sewing thread

Instructions

Center and stitch the Snowman Stocking or Snow Woman Stocking chart on *pages 67–68* on the Aida cloth. Use two plies of floss to work the stitches over one square of the fabric unless otherwise specified. Press the stitched piece from the back.

Center and fuse the fleece to the back of the stitched piece, following the manufacturer's instructions. Use the erasable fabric marker to draw the stocking outline as indicated by the dashed line on the chart. Cut out the stocking shape 1⁄2" beyond the marked outline.

Use the trimmed stitched piece as a pattern to cut a matching back and two lining pieces from the red fabric. From the remaining red fabric, cut a 1¼×5" hanging strip and enough 1¼"-wide bias strips to make a 36" length of piping.

Sew the short ends of the 1¼"-wide bias strips together to make a continuous length. Center the cording lengthwise on the wrong side of the piping strip. Fold the fabric around the cording, long edges even. Use a zipper foot to sew through both layers, close to the cording.

With raw edges even and using a zipper foot, baste the piping around the sides and foot of the stocking front. Sew the stocking front to the back, right sides together, along the basting lines, leaving the top edge open. Trim the seams and clip the curves. Turn the stocking right side out; press. Baste piping around the top edge of the stocking, raw edges even.

For the hanger, press under 3⁄8" along each long edge of the 1¼×5" hanger strip. Fold the strip in half lengthwise, aligning pressed edges; press again. Sew the long edges together opposite the fold. Fold the strip in half to form a loop. Baste the ends to the top outer corner on the heel side of the stocking.

With right sides facing, sew the lining pieces together with a 1⁄2" seam allowance, leaving the top edge open and an opening on one side for turning. Trim the seams and clip the curves; do not turn. Slip the stocking inside the lining, right sides together. Sew the top edges of the stocking and the lining together; turn right side out. Slip-stitch the opening closed. Tuck the lining into the stocking; press.

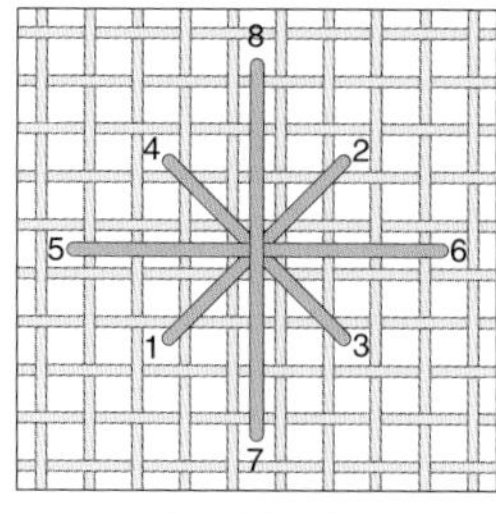

Star Stitch

Snowman Stocking Key

ANCHOR		DMC
CROSS-STITCH (3X)		
002	•	000 White
403	■	310 Black
400	=	317 Charcoal
351	☒	400 Mahogany
103	⁄	775 Light baby blue
1005	♥	816 Garnet
047	◙	817 Coral
332	✱	946 Burnt orange
244	▲	987 Forest green
292	+	3078 Topaz
328	◎	3341 Melon
1037	⊟	3756 Pale baby blue
BACKSTITCH (1X)		
351	/	400 Mahogany – birds' feet and beaks
1005	/	816 Garnet – scarf
403	/	310 Black – all other stitches
FRENCH KNOT (1X wrapped twice)		
403	●	310 Black – birds' eyes
STAR STITCH (1X)		
103	✳	775 Light baby blue – snowflakes
STRAIGHT STITCH (2X)		
1005	/	816 Garnet – scarf fringe

Stitch count: *103 high x 52 wide*

Finished design size:
14-count fabric – 7 3/8 x 3 3/4 inches

Snowman Stocking

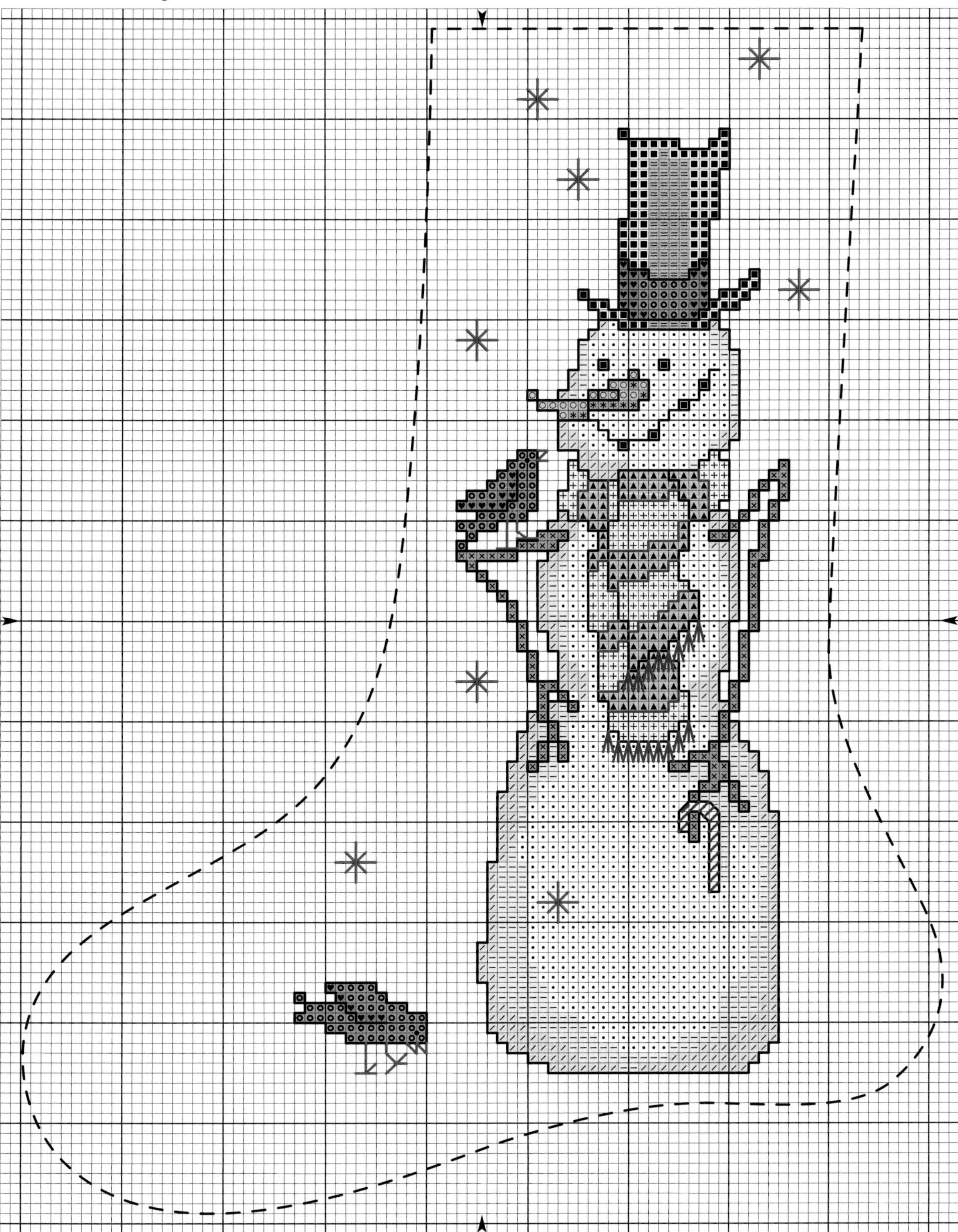

Snow Woman Stocking Key

ANCHOR DMC

CROSS-STITCH (3X)

ANCHOR	DMC
002	000 White
109	209 Medium lavender
403	310 Black
351	400 Mahogany
103	775 Light baby blue
1005	816 Garnet
047	817 Coral
332	946 Burnt orange
244	987 Forest green
433	996 Electric blue
292	3078 Topaz
328	3341 Melon
1037	3756 Pale baby blue
111	3837 Deep lavender

BACKSTITCH (1X)

ANCHOR	DMC
109	209 Medium lavender – feather plume
351	400 Mahogany – bird's feet and beak
403	310 Black – all other stitches

FRENCH KNOT (1X wrapped twice)

ANCHOR	DMC
403	310 Black – bird's eye

STAR STITCH (1X)

ANCHOR	DMC
103	775 Light baby blue – snowflakes

STRAIGHT STITCH (2X)

ANCHOR	DMC
111	3837 Deep lavender – scarf fringe

Stitch count: *101 high x 52 wide*

Finished design size:
14-count fabric – 7¹/₄ x 3³/₄ inches

Snow Woman Stocking

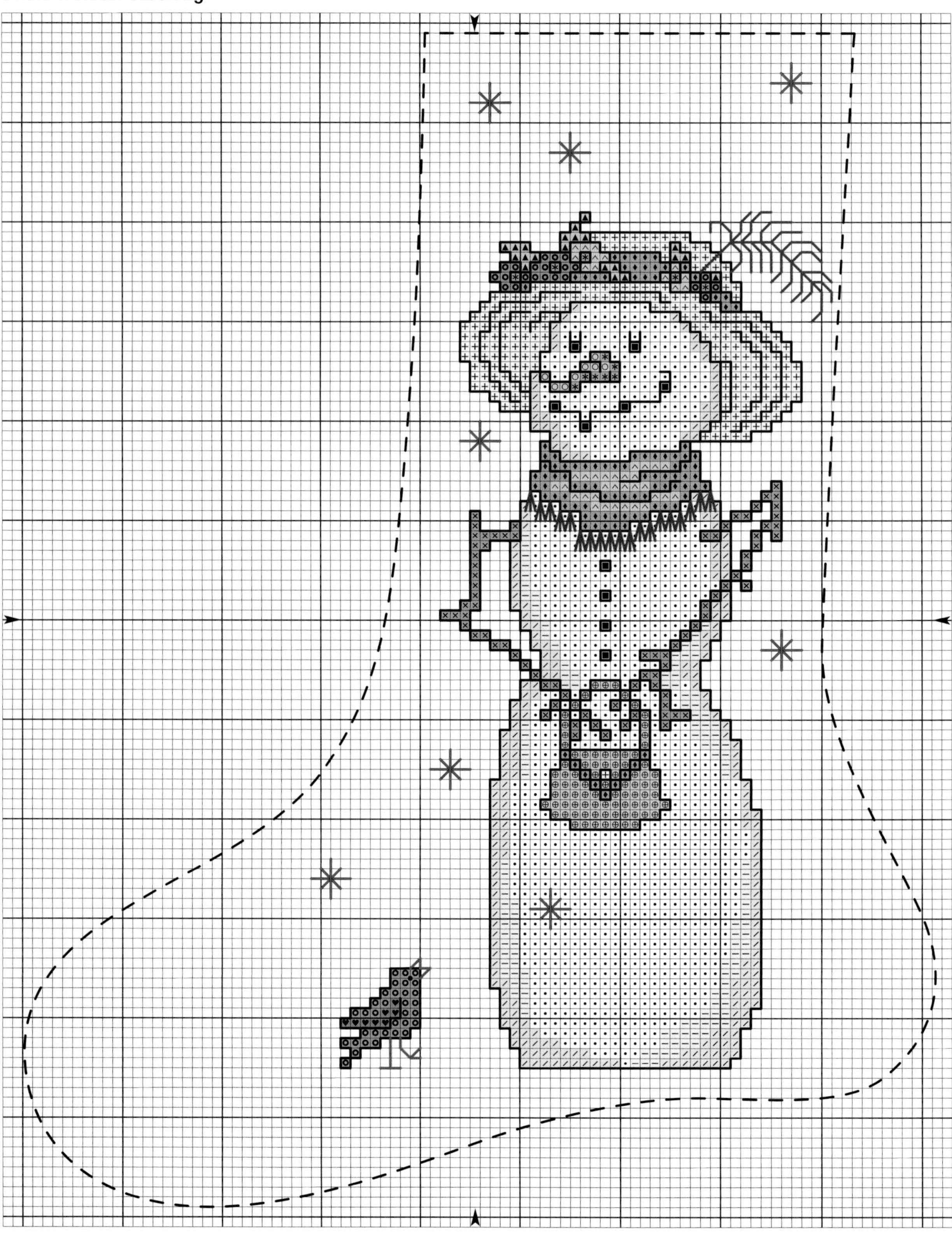

Let It Snow!

Materials

15" square of 14-count white Aida cloth
Cotton embroidery floss
Mill Hill beads
Desired frame

Instructions

Center and stitch the Let It Snow! chart on *page 70* on the Aida cloth. Use two plies of floss to work the stitches over one square of the fabric unless otherwise specified. Attach the beads using two plies of white floss. Place the finished piece facedown on a soft towel and carefully press from the back. Frame the piece as desired.

Snowman in the Woods

Materials

5" square of 40-count silk gauze
Kreinik Silk Mori floss
Desired frame

Instructions

Center and stitch the Snowman in the Woods chart on *page 71* on the silk gauze using tent stitches. Use one ply of silk floss to work stitches over one thread of gauze. Frame the piece as desired.

Snowman in the Woods Pillow

Materials

18" square piece of 7-count navy Klostern fabric
Cotton embroidery floss
½ yard of navy cotton fabric
1½ yard of ½"-diameter cording
Matching sewing thread
Polyester fiberfill
Red #5 pearl cotton
Embroidery needle

Instructions

Center and stitch the Snowman in the Woods chart on *page 71* on the Klostern fabric. Use six plies of floss to work the stitches over one square of the fabric unless otherwise specified. Press the stitched piece from the back.

Trim the stitched piece ½" beyond the outermost stitches. Use the trimmed stitched piece as a pattern to cut two matching shapes from the navy cotton fabric for a lining and back. From the remaining cotton fabric, cut enough 2"-wide bias strips to make a 50" length of piping. Sew all pieces with right sides together using ½" seams.

Sew the short ends of the 2"-wide bias strips together to make a continuous length. Center the cording lengthwise on the wrong side of the piping strip. Fold the fabric around the cording, long edges even. Use a zipper foot to sew through both layers, close to the cording.

Center the lining on the wrong side of the stitched piece and baste the layers together. With raw edges even, use a zipper foot to baste the piping around the perimeter of the pillow front. Sew the pillow front to the back along the basting lines, leaving an opening along the bottom for turning. Trim the seams. Turn the pillow right side out and press. Stuff the pillow firmly with polyester fiberfill. Slip-stitch the opening closed.

Thread an embroidery needle with red pearl cotton. Wrap the pearl cotton around the piping, bringing the needle through the piping at the inner edge every ½".

Let It Snow! Key

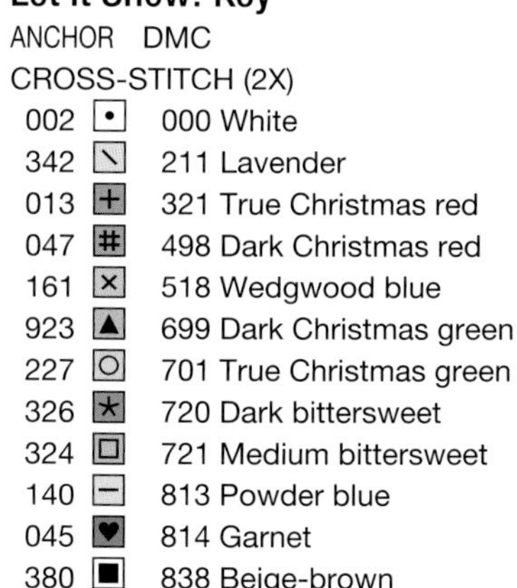

ANCHOR DMC

CROSS-STITCH (2X)

ANCHOR	Symbol	DMC
002	•	000 White
342	╲	211 Lavender
013	+	321 True Christmas red
047	#	498 Dark Christmas red
161	×	518 Wedgwood blue
923	▲	699 Dark Christmas green
227	○	701 True Christmas green
326	★	720 Dark bittersweet
324	□	721 Medium bittersweet
140	–	813 Powder blue
045	♥	814 Garnet
380	■	838 Beige-brown
1033	▽	932 Antique blue
048	|	963 Pink
1031	◇	3753 Cornflower blue
1037	^	3756 Baby blue

ANCHOR DMC

BACKSTITCH (1X)

ANCHOR	DMC
002	000 White – scarf stripes
161	518 Wedgwood blue – snowflakes, lettering
045	814 Garnet – scarf fringe
403	310 Black – all other stitches

MILL HILL BEAD

- 00143 Robin egg blue – border
- 02014 Black – snowman

Stitch count: *96 high x 102 wide*

Finished design size:
14-count fabric – 6 7/8 x 7 1/4 inches

Let It Snow!

Snowman in the Woods

Snowman in the Woods Key

ANCHOR		DMC	SILK MORI
CROSS-STITCH (3X)			
002	•	000 White	8000 White
403	■	310 Black	8050 Black
979	⊕	312 Navy	5095 Royal blue
013	◉	321 Christmas red	1114 Christmas red
398	☰	415 Pearl gray	8073 Charcoal
169	●	517 Dark Wedgwood blue	5105 Dark cerulean
161	+	518 Light Wedgwood blue	5104 Medium cerulean
227	–	701 True Christmas green	4036 Kelly green
239	×	702 Light Christmas green	4034 Medium kelly green
306	▽	729 Old gold	2015 Medium gold

ANCHOR		DMC	SILK MORI
CROSS-STITCH (3X)			
103	◇	775 Light baby blue	0523 Portsmouth blue
246	▲	986 Forest green	4037 Dark kelly green
075	○	3688 Medium mauve	1043 Cobalt violet
1037	⁄	3756 Pale baby blue	5091 Ice blue
069	♥	3803 Dark mauve	1046 Cobalt blue
891	⟍	3822 Light straw	2013 Light gold
308	★	3852 Deep straw	2016 Dark gold

Stitch count: *80 high x 80 wide*

Finished design size:
7-count fabric – 11 3/8 x 11 3/8 inches

Festive Greetings

Christmas is the time when we take special pleasure in handcrafting decorations and gifts, creating treasures from the heart for those we love. The country-style wall hanging at *right* will help set a casual tone for your holiday entertaining. Here and on the following pages, you'll find a varied collection of holiday crafts designed to lend beauty, elegance, and a rich charm to your holiday home.

Project instructions begin on page 80.

Design: Kathy Moenkhaus, Evening Star Designs • Photography: Hopkins Associates

may
you
know
joy
and
Love
at
hrist
mas

Christmas ushers in a season of merrymaking, fun, and informal get-togethers. You can easily make coordinating accessories by stitching one or more of the motifs from the Christmas Quilt Wall Hanging, as shown *above* and at *left*. Fashion quick ornaments, or stitch up a set of place mats using the motifs to create pieces that can be used year-round.

Project instructions begin on page 80.

Design: Kathy Moenkhaus, Evening Star Designs • Photography: Hopkins Associates

The sweet simplicity of this whimsical piece captures the essence of early country style. Subtle shading is achieved by stitching the piece with overdyed threads. Stitch the mittens, or add mitten buttons as shown at *right*.

Project instructions begin on page 82.

Design: Linda Ebright, Lizzie Kate • Photography: Perry Struse

Festive Greetings

Keep
Christmas
IN YOUR
Heart

Festive Greetings

The key to homespun country decor is simplicity. This rustic ornament *left* with its simple message of the season is sure to be a favorite. You'll want to stitch several of these charming ornaments to hang from the branches of your country-style tree.

Project instructions begin on page 82.
Design: Jan Fate • Photography: Hopkins Associates

This handsome wall hanging opposite will add country warmth to your home and extend a heartwarming welcome to your guests. The finishing is a breeze, too. Hand-sewn leather strips are attached to the piece, then tied around pieces of tree branches.

Project instructions begin on page 85.
Design: Barbara Peterson • Photography: Greg Scheidemann

The bright-eyed excitement exhibited during the holidays is a pleasure enjoyed by the child in each of us. But sometimes the anticipation of Santa's visit and the treasures he brings makes it difficult to resist peeking. Hang this playful ornament *left* on a cupboard or your tree as a gentle reminder.

Project instructions begin on page 82.
Design: Ann Pettit • Photography: Greg Scheidemann

Warmest
Wishes

Stitch this classic village scene *above* and capture its old-fashioned charm. The soft colors of the checkerboard border will lend a country hospitality to your home. If you find yourself running out of time, then you'll want to stitch up several of these festive ornaments *right.* It's hard to beat perforated plastic for quick and delightful Christmas ornaments. And the finishing is a snap! Graduated sizes of scrapbook papers are glued to the back of the piece. If you prefer to stitch on fabric, the Aida-cloth version gives you another finishing option.

Project instructions begin on page 87.

Design: Gail Bussi • Photography: Hopkins Associates, Greg Scheidemann

Festive Greetings

Add a clever touch to your gift giving with this cheerful stocking *right.* We've filled our stocking with candy, but it can hold a small package or treats of all kinds. Try stitching a row of the motifs on a higher-count fabric, then frame it for a unique decorative piece. Or choose a slightly richer color palette, then work the design over one thread of silk gauze to create a miniature version.

Project instructions begin on page 88.

Design: Alice Okon

Photography: Greg Scheidemann

Festive Greetings

Christmas Quilt Wall Hanging

Materials

12" square piece of 28-count lambswool Jobelan fabric
Cotton embroidery floss
1/3 yard of red cotton fabric
1/8 yard of green cotton fabric
13" square of lightweight quilt batting
Matching sewing thread
Three 3/4"-diameter dark green buttons
#5 cream pearl cotton
12"-long candy cane

Instructions

Center and stitch the Christmas Quilt Wall Hanging chart *opposite* on the Jobelan fabric. Use two plies of floss to work the stitches over two threads of the fabric unless otherwise specified. Press the stitched piece from the back.

Centering the design, trim the stitched piece to a 7¾" square. From the red fabric, cut four 3×7¾" sashing strips, three 4×6" hanging tabs, and a 13" square for the back. From the green fabric, cut four 3" squares. All measurements include a ½" seam allowance.

Sew a sashing strip to the left and right edges of the stitched piece; press the seam allowances toward the strips. Sew a 3" green square to each end of the remaining sashing strips; press the seam allowances toward the strips. Sew one pieced strip to the top of the stitched piece and one to the bottom, matching seams, to complete the wall-hanging front. Press seam allowances toward the sashing strips.

For each hanging tab, fold a 4×6" piece in half to measure 2×6". Sew the long edge and one short edge together. Trim the seams, turn the tabs right side out, and press. With raw edges even, position the tabs on the right side of the wall-hanging front, placing a tab 1" from each top corner and at the top center. Baste the tabs to the front.

Place the quilt batting on a flat surface. Center and smooth the back, right side up, on the batting. Center and smooth the wall-hanging front, right side down, on the back. Pin-baste all layers together. Sew the layers together ½" from the edges of the front, leaving an opening along the bottom for turning. Trim the back and batting even with the front. Turn the wall hanging right side out. Slip-stitch the opening closed.

Fold the tabs down even with the top of the wall hanging. Center a button on the front of each tab about ¼" above the wall hanging. Use pearl cotton to attach the buttons, knotting the pearl cotton on the front of each button. Insert the candy cane through the tab.

Note: We used a real candy cane for our photography. For a longer lasting way to display your wall hanging, you could paint a large dowel to resemble a candy cane.

Christmas Quilt Place Mat

Materials

Purchased 13×18" 14-count country oatmeal place mat
Cotton embroidery floss

Instructions

Begin stitching the bottom left corner of the Christmas Quilt Wall Hanging chart *opposite* in the bottom left corner of the place mat, 1½" in from the fringed edges. Use three plies of floss to work the stitches over one square of the fabric. Stitch the checkerboard border and house motif, stopping the border 1" from the top fringed edge of the place mat and at the right edge of the house.

Referring to the photograph on *page 74* and working up from the house motif, stitch the pinwheel motif, the flying geese motif, and the star motif, leaving 20 squares between each motif. Press the finished place mat from the back.

Christmas Quilt Napkin

Materials

Purchased 15" square 14-count country oatmeal napkin
Cotton embroidery floss

Instructions

Stitch the star motif from the Christmas Wall Hanging chart *opposite* in one corner of the napkin, 1½" in from the fringed edges. Use three plies of floss to work the stitches over one square of the fabric. Press the finished napkin from the back.

Christmas Quilt Wall Hanging Key

ANCHOR	DMC
CROSS-STITCH (2X)	
020	221 Deep shell pink
019	304 Christmas red
217	367 Pistachio
862	520 Deep olive drab
860	522 Dark olive drab
045	814 Dark garnet
1005	816 Light garnet
862	934 Pine green
817	3345 Hunter green
261	3363 Loden

ANCHOR	DMC
CROSS-STITCH (2X)	
896	3721 Dark shell pink
1015	3777 Terra-cotta
BACKSTITCH (1X)	
382	3371 Black-brown

Quilt stitch count: *88 high x 88 wide*
Quilt finished design size:
28-count fabric – 6 1/4 x 6 1/4 inches
Ornament stitch count: *20 high x 20 wide*
Ornament finished design size:
14-count fabric – 1 3/8 x 1 3/8 inches

Christmas Quilt Wall Hanging

Keep Christmas in Your Heart

Materials

17×18" piece of 26-count navy Heatherfield fabric
Sampler Threads overdyed floss
Two 1⅛"-tall mitten buttons
Two ⅛"-diameter white buttons
5½" length of ⅛"-wide green satin ribbon
Desired frame

Instructions

Center and stitch the Keep Christmas in Your Heart chart *opposite* on the fabric. Use two plies of floss to work the stitches over two threads of the fabric unless otherwise specified. When working with overdyed threads, work each cross-stitch completely before continuing to the next stitch. Press the finished piece from the back.

Use two plies of floss to attach the beads and buttons at the marks indicated on chart. Tie the ribbon into a bow. Tack the center of the bow to the candy cane. Trim the ribbon ends. Frame the piece as desired.

Noel Ornament

Materials

28-count natural linen: 9" square for front and 4¾" square for back
Cotton embroidery floss
Polyester fiberfill
8" length of fine twine

Instructions

Center and stitch the Noel Ornament chart on *page 84* on the linen. Use two plies of floss to work the stitches over two threads of the fabric unless otherwise specified. Press the stitched piece from the back.

Centering the design, trim the stitched piece into a 4¾" square, rounding the corners. Place the stitched piece right side up on the back square. Round the corners of the back square to match the front. Sew the ornament front to the back ¼" from the edges with running stitches, using one ply of black floss (DMC 310) and leaving a 2½" opening centered along the top edge. Do not cut the floss at this time.

Lightly stuff the ornament with the polyester fiberfill. For the hanging loop, insert the ends of the twine into the ornament at the ends of the opening. Continue working the running stitches to close the opening, catching the twine in the stitches.

No Peeking Door Hanger

Materials

9×8" piece of 30-count light espresso linen
Cotton embroidery floss
Kreinik blending filament
2⅛×3¼" rectangle of lightweight cardboard
2⅛×3¼" rectangle of fleece
Crafts glue
2×3⅛" rectangle of felt
Two small rose quartz beads

Instructions

Center and stitch the No Peeking chart on *page 84* on the linen. Use one ply of floss to work the stitches over one thread of the fabric unless otherwise specified. Press the stitched piece from the back.

Centering the design, trim the stitched piece to measure 4×3". Center and glue the fleece to the cardboard rectangle.

Center the stitched piece, wrong side down, on the fleece. Fold the edges of the stitched piece to the back and glue in place. Glue the felt to the ornament back.

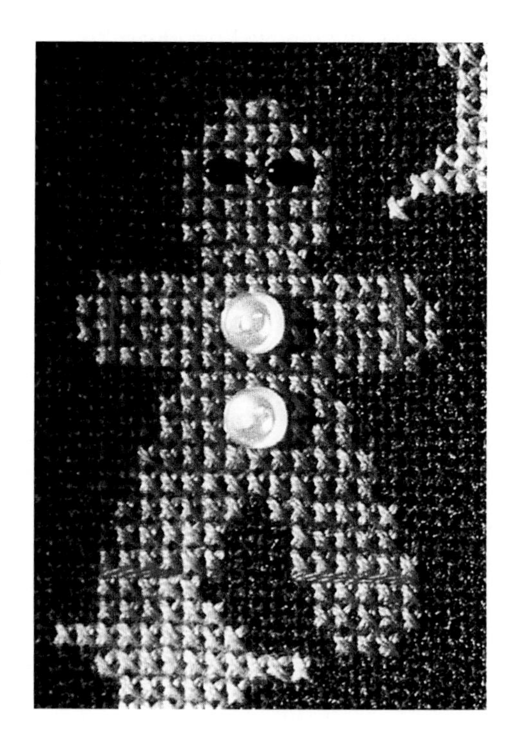

For the twisted cord, cut two 68" lengths *each* of Medium shell pink (DMC 223) and Dark olive drab (DMC 522). Combine the cut lengths into a single strand and tie a knot in each end. Secure one knot to a stationary object and twist the opposite end until the floss is very tightly twisted and begins to kink. Holding the ends, fold the stand in half and allow the two halves to twist around each other. Make a knot ¼" from each end; then cut the folded end to fringe.

Beginning with a 1"-long tail at the top right corner, hand-sew the twisted cord to the edges of the door hanger. To create a hanging loop, position the end of the twisted cord at the top left corner of the ornament. Sew a rose quartz bead over the cord 1" from the knot. Sew the second bead over the cord at the top right corner in the same manner.

Keep Christmas in Your Heart Key

Anchor	DMC		Sampler Threads
1006	304	♡	Cherry wine
978	322	×	Bluejay
212	561	▲	Pine
926	712	–	Oatmeal
890	729	☆	Gold leaf
355	975	+	Nutmeg
1030	3746	#	Purple iris

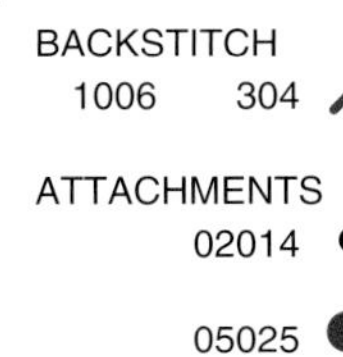

BACKSTITCH

1006 304 / Cherrywine – gingerbread boy (2X)

ATTACHMENTS

02014 ● Mill Hill Black seed beads – eyes

05025 ● Red pebble beads – berries

× Bow placement

× Mitten buttons

× ⅛"-diameter White buttons – gingerbread boy

Stitch count: *90 high x 86 wide*

Finished design sizes:
26-count fabric – 6⅞ x 6⅝ inches
28-count fabric – 6⅜ x 6⅛ inches
32-count fabric – 5⅝ x 5⅜ inches

Keep Christmas in Your Heart

No Peeking Door Hanger

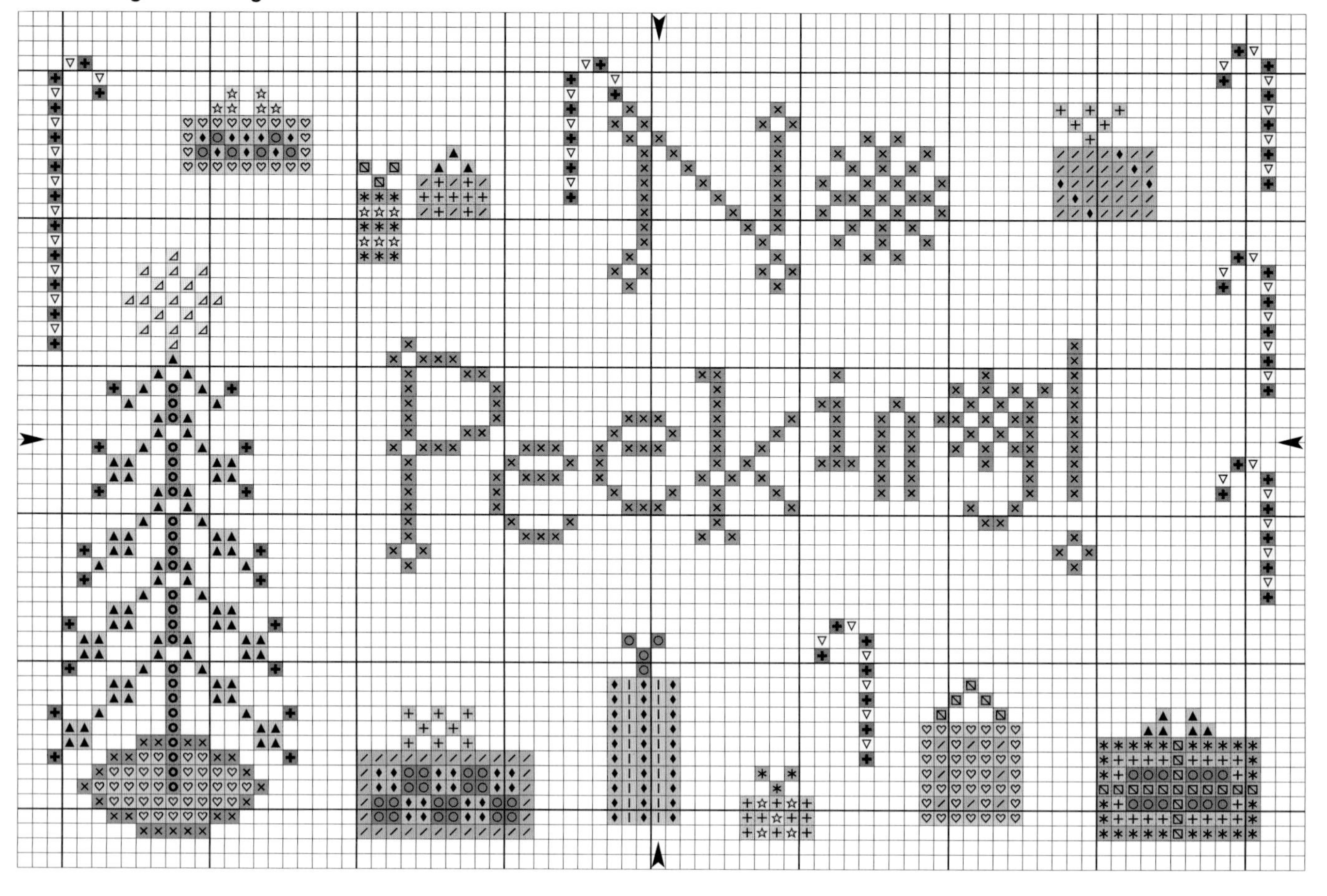

No Peeking Door Hanger Key

ANCHOR DMC

CROSS-STITCH (1X)

- 926 Ecru
- 894 152 Bright shell pink
- 020 221 Deep shell pink
- 895 223 Medium shell pink
- 893 224 Light shell pink
- 860 522 Dark olive drab
- 889 610 Deep drab brown
- 306 729 Medium old gold
- 843 3013 Khaki
- 859 3053 Light gray-green
- 262 3362 Loden
- 896 3721 Dark shell pink
- 1027 3722 True shell pink
- 1018 3726 Antique mauve

BLENDED NEEDLE CROSS-STITCH

- 874 676 Light old gold (1X) and 002HL Kreinik Gold hi lustre blending filament

Stitch count: *53 high x 82 wide*

Finished design size:
30-count fabric – $1^3/_4$ x $2^3/_4$ inches

Noel Tree Ornament

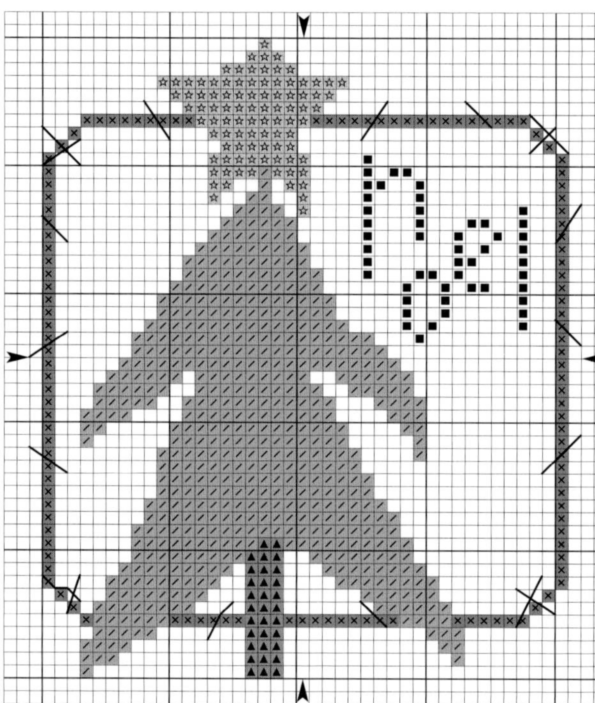

Noel Tree Ornament Key

ANCHOR DMC

CROSS-STITCH (2X)

- 352 300 Mahogany
- 403 310 Black
- 047 498 Christmas red
- 683 500 Blue-green
- 307 783 Christmas gold

STRAIGHT STITCH (1X)

- 403 310 Black

Stitch count: *50 high x 43 wide*

Finished design size:
28-count fabric – $3^5/_8$ x $3^1/_8$ inches

Warmest Wishes

Materials

13×14" piece of 28-count natural brown linen
Cotton embroidery floss
Kreinik blending filament
8½×9" piece each of mounting board and quilt batting
Spray adhesive
Thick white crafts glue
8×8½" piece of white felt
Leather strips: five ½×10" and one ½×15"
Matching sewing thread
Hand-sewing needle
Two 10" lengths of ⅞"-diameter tree branch

Instructions

Center and stitch the Warmest Wishes chart on *page 86* on the linen. Use three plies of floss to work the stitches over two threads of the fabric unless otherwise specified. Press the stitched piece from the back.

Centering the design, trim the stitched piece into a 10½×11" rectangle. Spray one side of the mounting board with adhesive. Immediately center and smooth the quilt batting onto the adhesive side of the board. Center the batting side of the mounting board on the back of the stitched piece. Fold fabric edges to the back, mitering the corners to reduce bulk; glue in place. Center and glue the felt rectangle on the back.

Position the center of three 10"-long strips on the bottom edge of the stitched piece, placing one at the center and one 1¼" from each corner. Hand-sew the strips in place. For the top edge, position the 15" strip at the center and a 10" strip 1¼" from each top corner. Sew the strips in place. Knot the leather strips around each branch. For the hanging loop, tie a knot in the ends of the top center strip.

Warmest Wishes

ANCHOR	DMC
CROSS-STITCH (3X)	
1049	301 Medium mahogany
853	372 Pecan
371	433 Caramel
1040	647 Beaver gray
234	762 Pearl gray
1005	816 Garnet
381	938 Coffee brown
262	3362 Dark loden
260	3364 Light loden
1048	3776 True mahogany
306	3820 Straw
BLENDED NEEDLE CROSS-STITCH	
002	000 White (2X) and 032 Kreinik Pearl blending filament (2X)
HALF CROSS-STITCH (3X) (stitch in direction of symbols)	
858	524 Olive drab
BACKSTITCH (1X)	
381	938 Coffee brown – all stitches

Stitch count: *110 high x 106 wide*

Finished design size:
28-count fabric – 7⅞ x 7½ inches

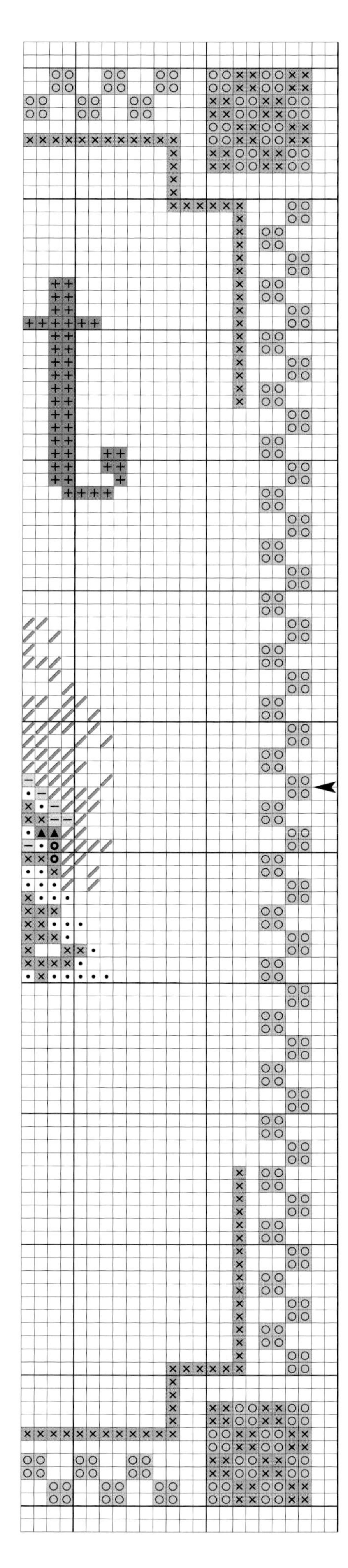

Festive Greetings

Christmas in the Country

Materials

10×14" piece of 32-count flax Belfast linen
Cotton embroidery floss
Desired frame

Instructions

Center and stitch the Christmas in the Country chart on *pages 90–91* on the fabric. Use two plies of floss to work the stitches over two threads of the fabric unless otherwise specified. Press the stitched piece from the back. Frame the piece as desired.

Christmas in the Country Paper Ornaments

Materials

For each ornament:
3" square of 14-count white perforated plastic
Cotton embroidery floss
Five coordinating sheets of paper, including white
Pinking shears
Two coordinating colors of #5 pearl cotton
Crafts glue

Instructions

Center and stitch the desired motif from the Christmas in the Country chart on *pages 90–91* onto the perforated plastic. Use three plies of floss to work the stitches unless otherwise specified.

Trim the stitched piece one square beyond the stitched area. Cut a piece of white paper the same size as the trimmed stitchery. From the four remaining papers, cut progressively larger rectangles, using pinking shears to cut one of the layers if you like.

For the twisted cording hanger, cut a 24" length of each pearl cotton. Combine the cut lengths into a single strand and tie a knot in each end. Secure one knot to a stationary object and twist the opposite end until the pearl cotton is very tightly twisted and begins to kink. Holding the ends, fold the strands in half and allow the two halves to twist around each other. Make knots in the cording 6" apart; trim the excess cording beyond the knots. Glue the knots at the top center on the front of the largest paper rectangle. Center and glue the rectangles from smallest to largest on the ornament back.

Christmas in the Country Fabric Ornaments

Materials

For each ornament:
8" square of 14-count light blue Aida cloth
Cotton embroidery floss
3¼"-diameter circle of self-stick mounting board with foam
Thick white crafts glue
4"-diameter circle of teal card stock
Decorative-edge scissors
8" length of ⅜"-wide sheer white ribbon

Instructions

Center and stitch the desired motif from the Christmas in the Country chart on *pages 91–92* onto the Aida cloth. Use three plies of floss to work the cross-stitches. Use one ply of floss to backstitch and to make star stitches and French knots. Press the stitched piece from the back.

Peel the protective paper backing from the mounting board. Center the foam side on the back of the stitched piece; press firmly to apply. Trim fabric to ½" beyond the edge of the mounting board. Fold fabric edges to the back, mitering the corners; glue in place.

Trim the edges of the card-stock circle with the decorative-edge scissors. Center and glue the card-stock circle on the ornament back. Fold the ribbon length in half to form a loop. Glue the ribbon ends to the center top on the ornament back. Let the glue dry.

Holiday Stocking Ornament

Materials

- 10×14" piece of 10-count cream Tula fabric
- Cotton embroidery floss
- 8×12" piece of fusible fleece
- Erasable fabric marker
- ⅓ yard of red cotton fabric
- Matching sewing threads
- ¾ yard of ¼"-diameter cording
- 1⅔ yards each of ⅛"-wide red, white, and green satin ribbon
- Clear tape
- ⅝"-diameter button
- 3¼"-long red tassel

Instructions

Center and stitch the Holiday Stocking chart *opposite* on the Tula fabric. Use six plies of floss to work the cross-stitches over one square of fabric. Backstitch with two plies of floss. Press the stitched piece from the back.

Center and fuse the fleece to the back of the stitched piece, following the manufacturer's instructions. Use the erasable fabric marker to draw the stocking outline as indicated by the dashed line on the chart. Cut out the stocking shape ½" beyond the marked outline.

Use the trimmed stitched piece as a pattern to cut a matching back and two lining pieces from the red fabric. From the remaining red fabric, cut enough 1¾"-wide bias strips to make a 27" length of piping.

Sew the short ends of the 1¾"-wide bias strips together to make a continuous length. Center the cording lengthwise on the wrong side of the piping strip. Fold the fabric around the cording, long edges even. Use a zipper foot to sew through both layers, close to the cording.

With raw edges even and using a zipper foot, baste the piping around the sides and foot of the stocking front, right sides together. Sew the stocking front to the back, right sides together, along the basting lines, leaving the top edge open. Trim the seams and clip the curves. Turn the stocking right side out; press.

For the braid trim, cut each ribbon length in half. Align the same color ribbon lengths and treat each color as one. Knot the lengths together at one end and braid the entire length of the ribbons. For the hanging loop, cut a 7" length of braid and wrap tape around the cut ends to secure. Fold the braid in half to form a loop. Sew the ends to the top outer corner on the heel side of the stocking. Tape the cut ends of the remaining braid and set aside.

With right sides facing, sew the lining pieces together with a ½" seam allowance, leaving the top edge open and an opening in one side for turning. Trim the seams and clip the curves; do not turn. Slip the stocking inside the lining, right sides together. Sew the top edges of the stocking and lining together. Remove the tape from the hanging loop ends. Turn the stocking right side out; slip-stitch the opening closed. Tuck the lining inside the stocking; press.

Hand-sew the set-aside braid along the top edge of the stocking, tucking the ends into the stocking at the heel seam and trimming the excess. Sew the button to the top right corner of the stocking front. Hang the tassel on the button.

Holiday Stocking Ornament Key

ANCHOR		DMC
CROSS-STITCH (6X)		
013	×	321 Christmas red
046	○	666 Red
228	●	700 Medium Christmas green
239	+	702 Light Christmas green
237	−	703 Chartreuse
1005	▲	816 Garnet
035	I	3705 Watermelon
BACKSTITCH (6X)		
013	/	321 Christmas red – berries
923	/	699 Dark Christmas green – greenery
382	/	3371 Black-brown – all other stitches

Stitch count: *91 high x 55 wide*

Finished design size:
10-count fabric – 8 x 5½ inches

Holiday Stocking Ornament

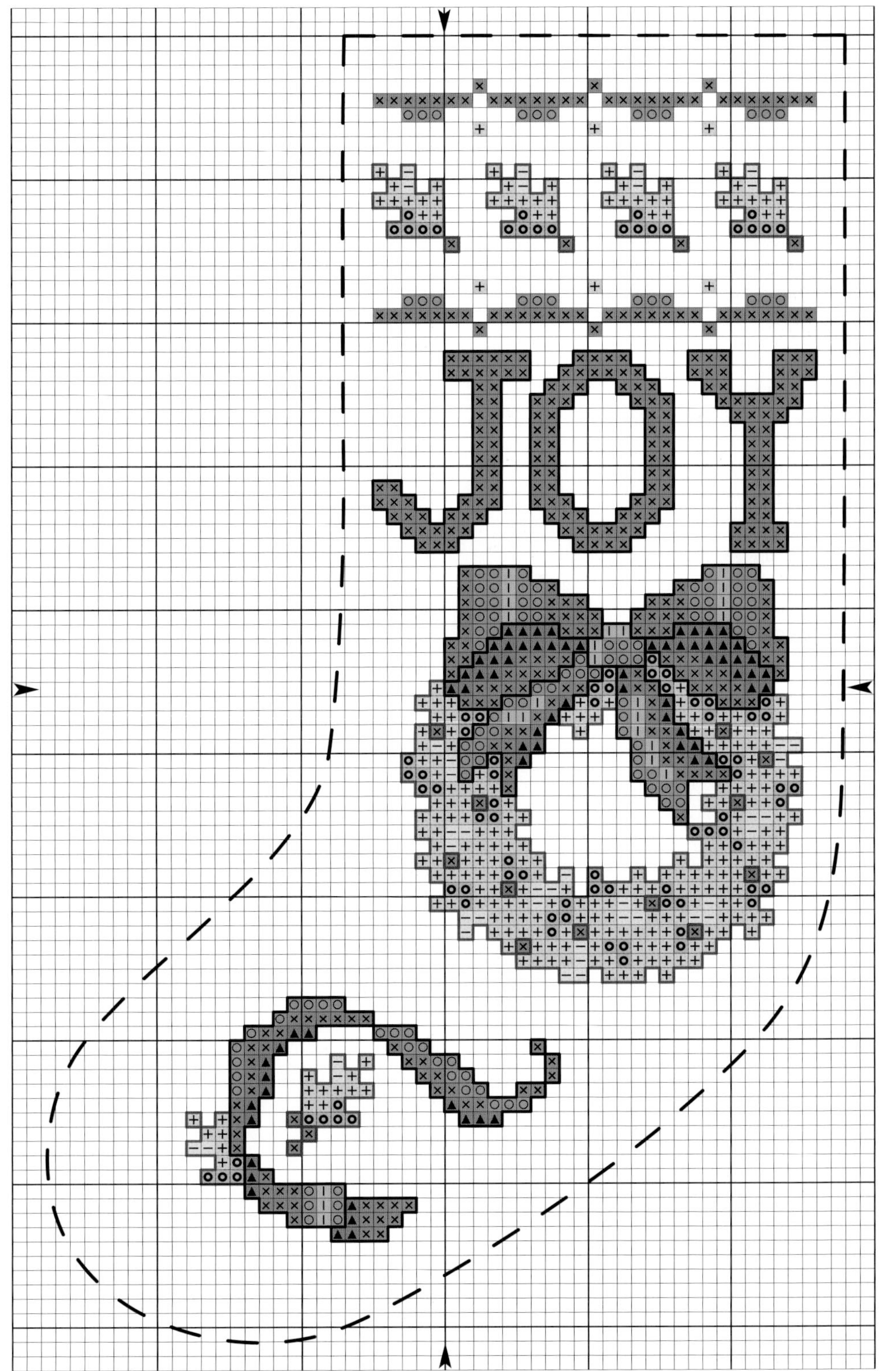

Christmas in the Country

Festive Greetings

Christmas in the Country Key

ANCHOR		DMC
CROSS-STITCH (2X)		
002	•	000 White
879	●	501 Dark blue-green
876	–	503 True blue-green
856	♦	611 Pecan
854	○	612 Drab brown
874	▽	676 Light old gold
390	I	822 Pale beige-gray
899	/	3782 Light mocha
1086	▲	3790 Dark beige-gray
877	×	3815 Celadon green
042	◉	3831 Dark raspberry
039	+	3832 Medium raspberry
BLENDED NEEDLE CROSS-STITCH		
002	☆	000 White (2X) and 100 Kreinik white blending filament (1X)
BACKSTITCH (1X)		
683	/	500 Deep blue-green – vines and lettering
042	/	3831 Dark raspberry – heart outline
381	/	3031 Deep mocha – all other stitches
RUNNING STITCH		
683	/	500 Deep blue-green – border
ALGERIAN EYELET (1X over 4 threads)		
306	✳	729 Medium old gold
FRENCH KNOT (1X wrapped twice)		
879	●	501 Dark blue-green – lettering, wreath on church and trees in windows
381	●	3031 Deep mocha – door knobs
042	●	3831 Dark raspberry – wreath on church

Stitch count: *61 high x 122 wide*

Finished design size:
32-count fabric – 3 7/8 x 7 5/8 inches

Come Home to Christmas

What a delight to share the joy of Christmas with those we love. The house is trimmed from top to bottom, heavenly aromas fill the air, and the whole family gathers together. Another joy is the giving and receiving of specially chosen—and perhaps specially handcrafted—gifts. Maybe it will be one of the designs on the following pages.

Project instructions begin on page 100.

Design: Emie Bishop • Photography: Hopkins Associates

JOY

I
Christmas

Come Home to Christmas

Dress a table or buffet with a tiny forest of stitched trees nestled in a bed of greens, *right.* We've inserted dowels into foam blocks to stand them up, but you could easily turn them into ornaments by adding a ribbon hanger. Best of all, you don't need to spend days stitching. You can be gifting your loved ones with handcrafted ornaments quicker than you can say "Merry Christmas."

Project instructions begin on page 104.
Design: Gail Bussi • Photography: Dean Tanner

This lacy and elegant design *opposite* features a Hardanger heart alongside a familiar saying for this time of year. Expand your stitching knowledge by learning a few Hardanger stitches that you can use to create delicate accessories year-round.

Project instructions begin on page 102.
Design: Donna Yuen • Photography: Perry Struse

These tiny stockings *above* work up in no time at all. We've stitched them in several color options, but you could easily change the colors to suit your tastes.

Project instructions begin on page 106.

Design: Alice Okon • Photography: Hopkins Associates

Seasonal motifs combine beautifully to create this lovely sampler *opposite*. We've shown the design in shades of blue, but because the design uses only three colors, you can easily substitute ones that coordinate with those in your home.

Project instructions begin on page 106.

Design: Laura Holtorf Collins • Photography: Hopkins Associates

ABCDEFGHIJKLM
NOPQRSTUVWXYZ

Cross-stitched patches along with button and ribbon embellishments add a special charm to this engaging pair. Our Rag Bag Santa and Believe Angel *above* are certain to bring smiles to those who see them.

Project instructions begin on page 110.

Design: Gail Bussi • Photography: Greg Scheidemann

Come Home to Christmas

Santa Claus, Saint Nicholas, Sinter Klaus—no matter what name you call him or what style his cap and coat, he's always in style at Christmas. The Americana Santa on this whimsical stocking *opposite* is dressed in patriotic splendor and certain to become a family favorite.

Project instructions begin on page 110.

Design: Robin Clark • Photography: Hopkins Associates

BETSY

Come Home to Christmas

Holiday Joy

Materials

16×22" piece of 28-count cream Cashel linen
Cotton embroidery floss
#8 and #12 pearl cotton
Tapestry needle
Needlework frame
Desired frame and mat

Instructions

Measure 4" from the edges on one corner of the fabric; begin stitching the top row of the holly leaf from the Holiday Joy chart *right* in the corresponding corner there. Use two plies of floss to work the cross-stitches over two threads of the fabric. Work the backstitches using one ply of floss. Use one strand of #8 pearl cotton to work the satin stitches over the number of threads indicated on the chart.

Refer to the diagrams *opposite* to work the remaining stitches. Using #8 pearl cotton, work all Kloster blocks. Refer to the Removing Threads diagram and cut away the threads for the woven bar areas.

Using #12 pearl cotton and referring to the Needleweaving diagram, work the needleweaving over the exposed thread groups. Use one strand of #12 pearl cotton to work a dove's eye in the center of the openwork areas indicated on the chart. Referring to the Four-Sided Stitch diagram, use one strand of #12 pearl cotton to work the four-sided stitches. Press the finished piece from the back. Frame the piece as desired.

Holiday Joy

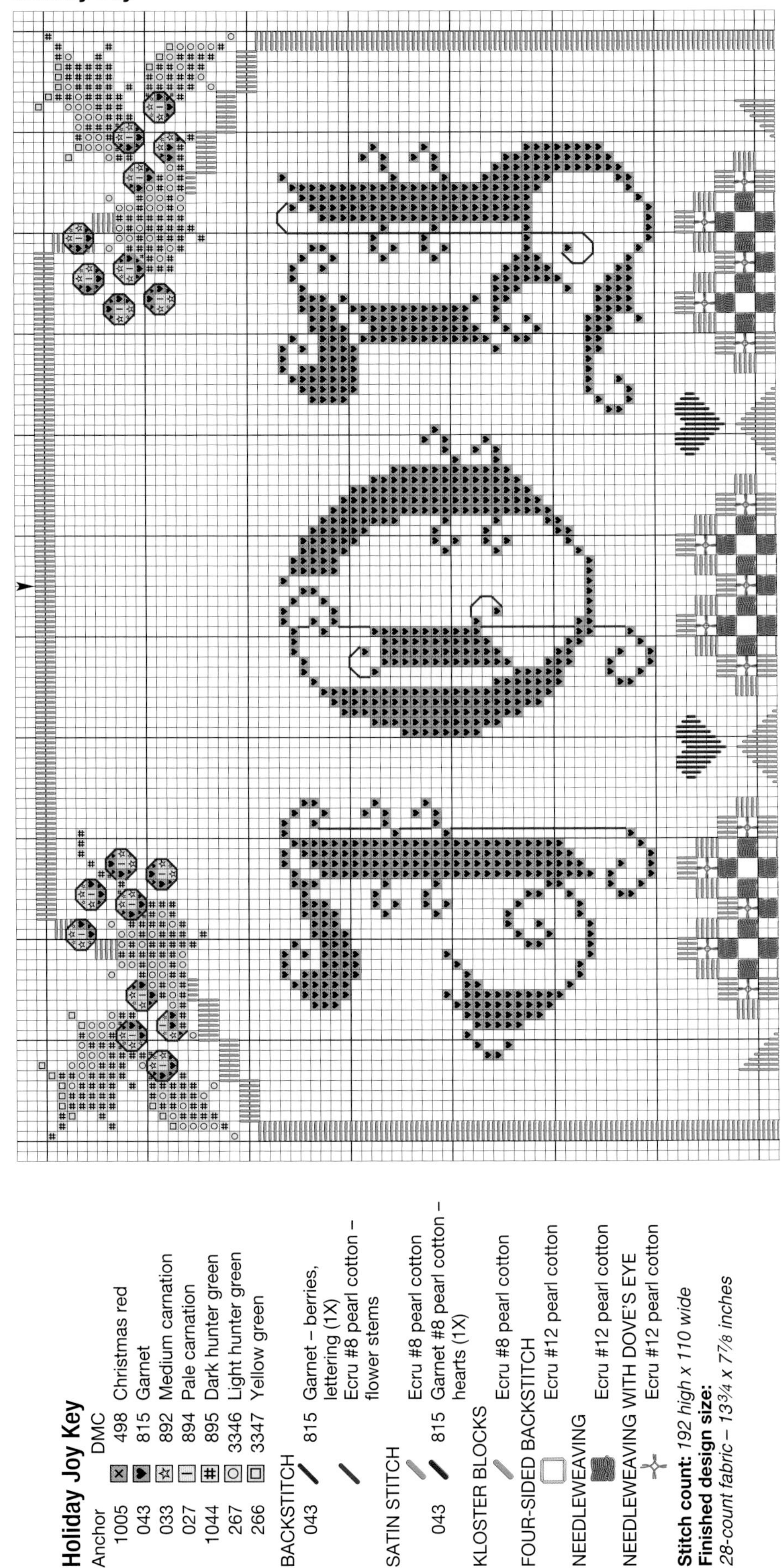

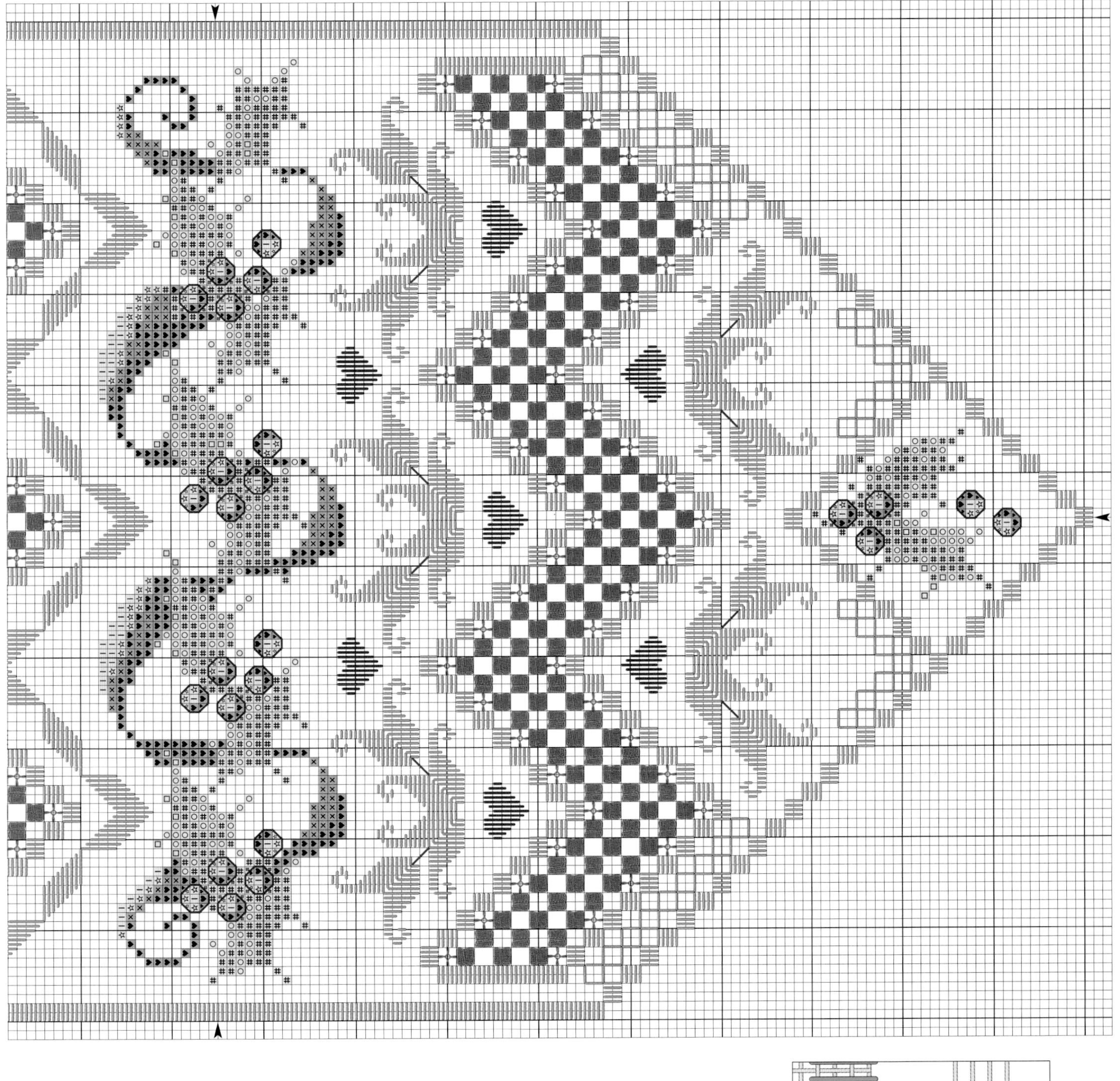

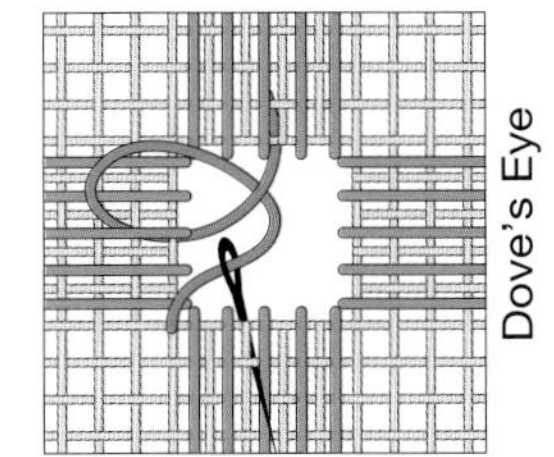
Dove's Eye

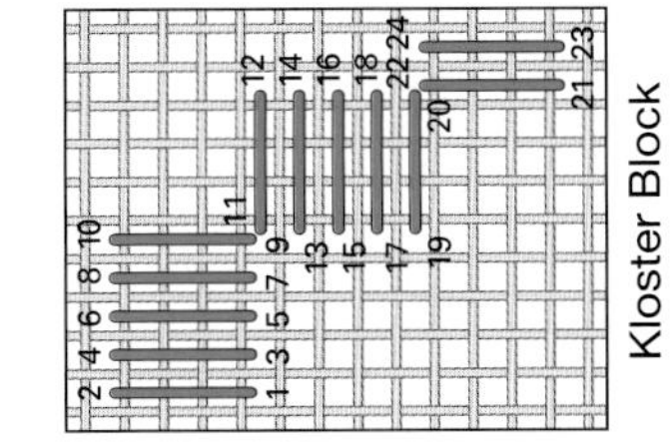
Kloster Block

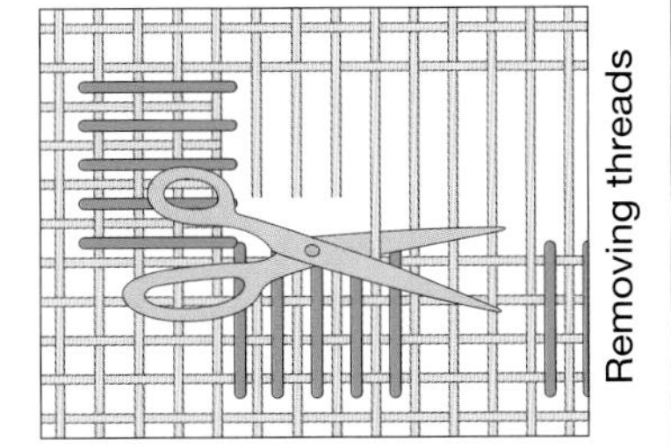
Removing threads

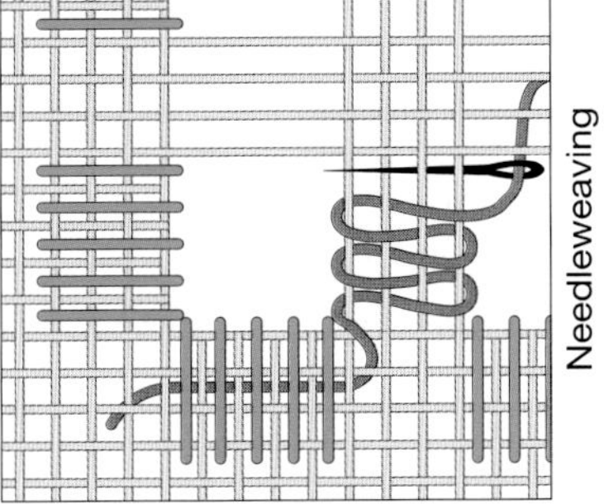
Needleweaving

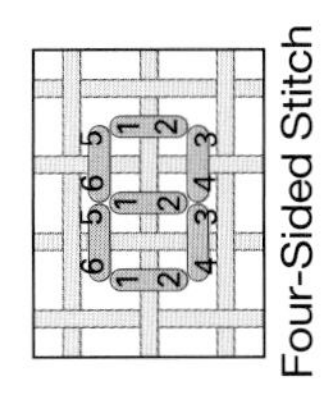
Four-Sided Stitch

I Love Christmas

Materials

18×20" piece of 25-count driftwood Dublin linen
Cotton embroidery floss
#5 and #12 pearl cotton
Mill Hill seed beads

Instructions

Center and stitch the I Love Christmas chart *opposite* on the fabric. First, use three plies of floss to work the cross-stitches over two threads of fabric. Then work the backstitches, satin stitches including Kloster blocks, wave-filling stitches, and eyelets using floss as specified or one strand of pearl cotton. Refer to the diagrams at *right* to work the specialty stitches.

Carefully cut and remove the threads. Thread a needle with a 30" length of #12 pearl cotton. Work the needleweaving stitches. Attach the seed beads using two plies of floss. Place the finished stitchery facedown on a soft towel and press from the back. Frame the piece as desired.

Come Home to Christmas

Needleweaving with Dove's Eye

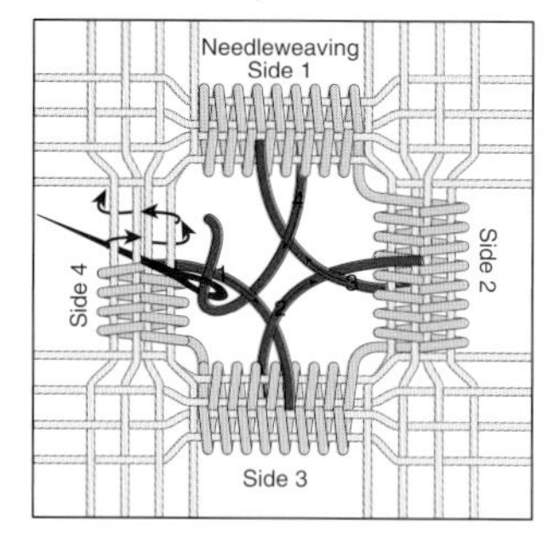

Cutting

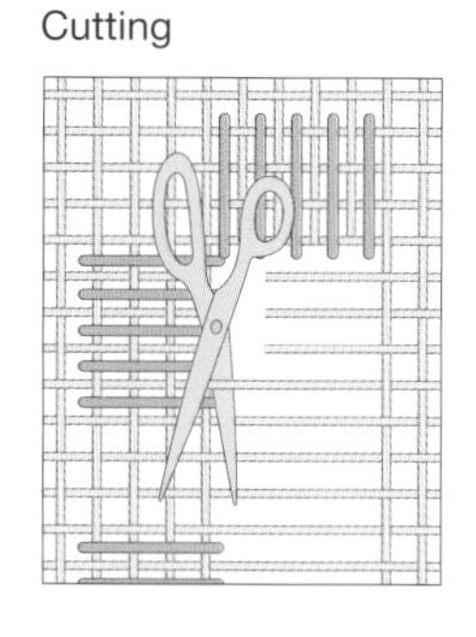

Needleweaving

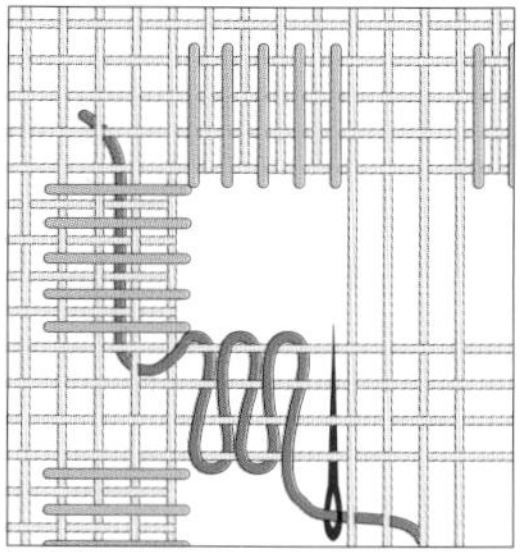

Needleweaving with Picots

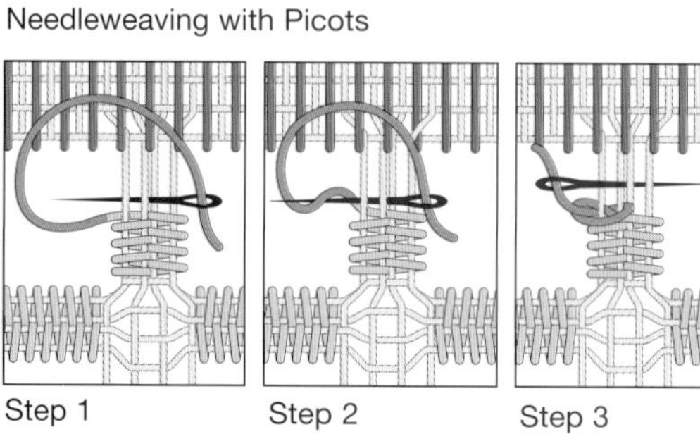

Step 1 Step 2 Step 3

Kloster Block

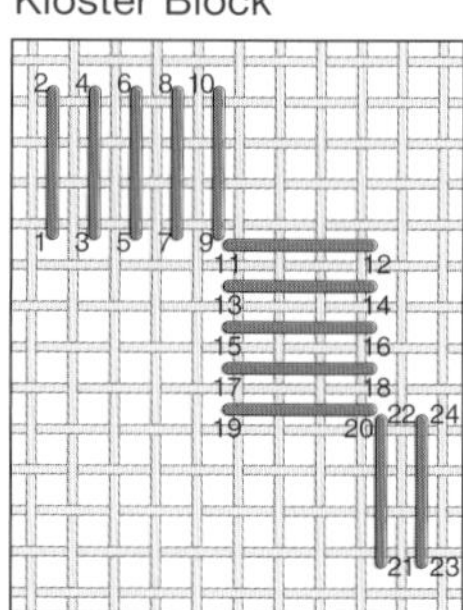

Wave-Filling Stitch

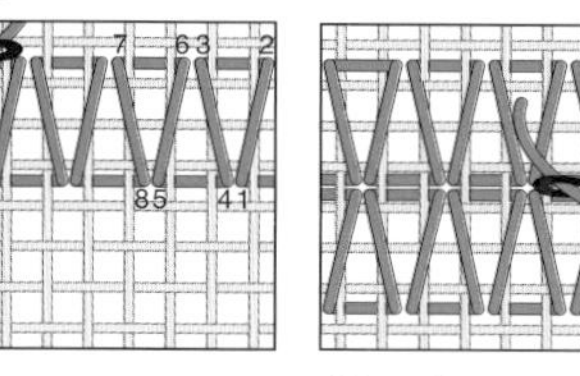

Step 1 Step 2

Cross Eyelet

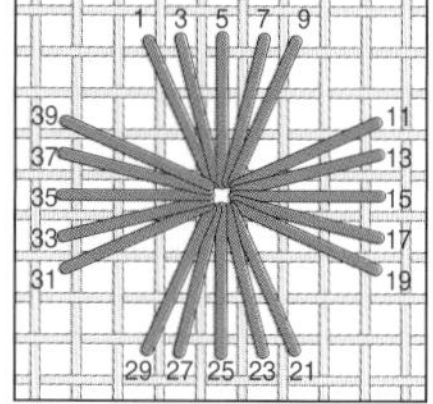

Needleweaving with Web

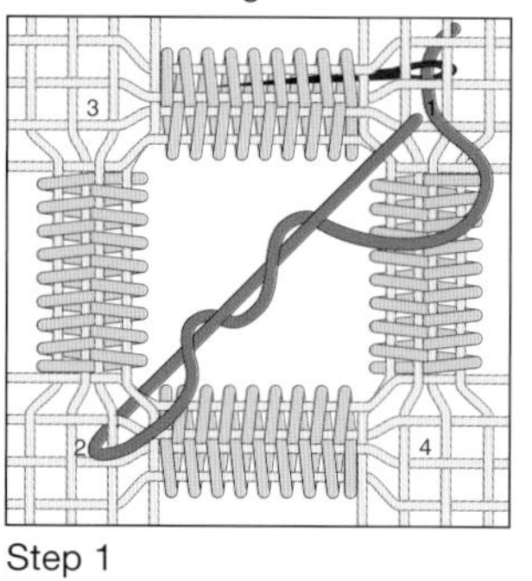

Step 1

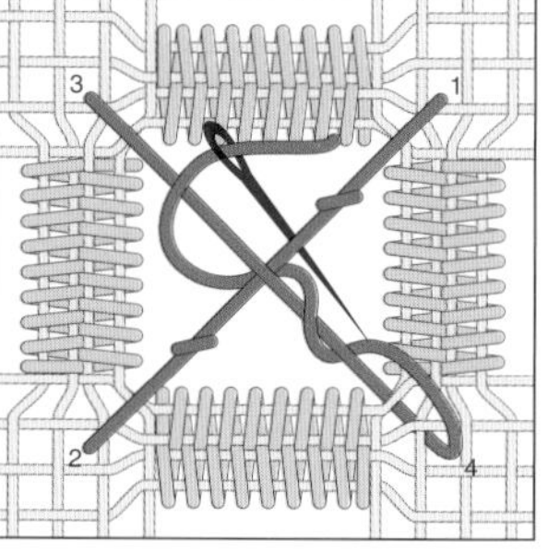

Step 2

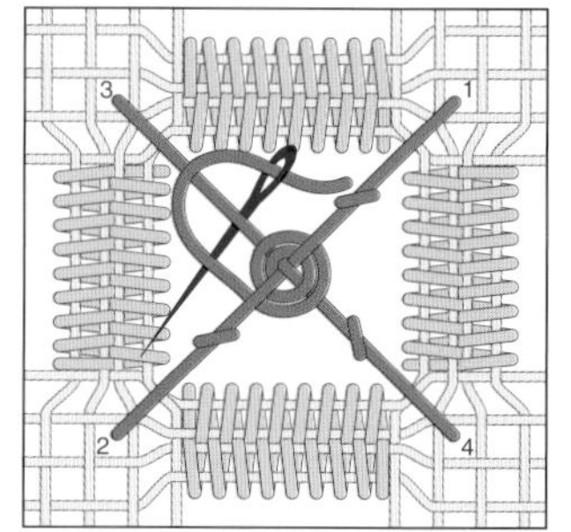

Step 3

I Love Christmas

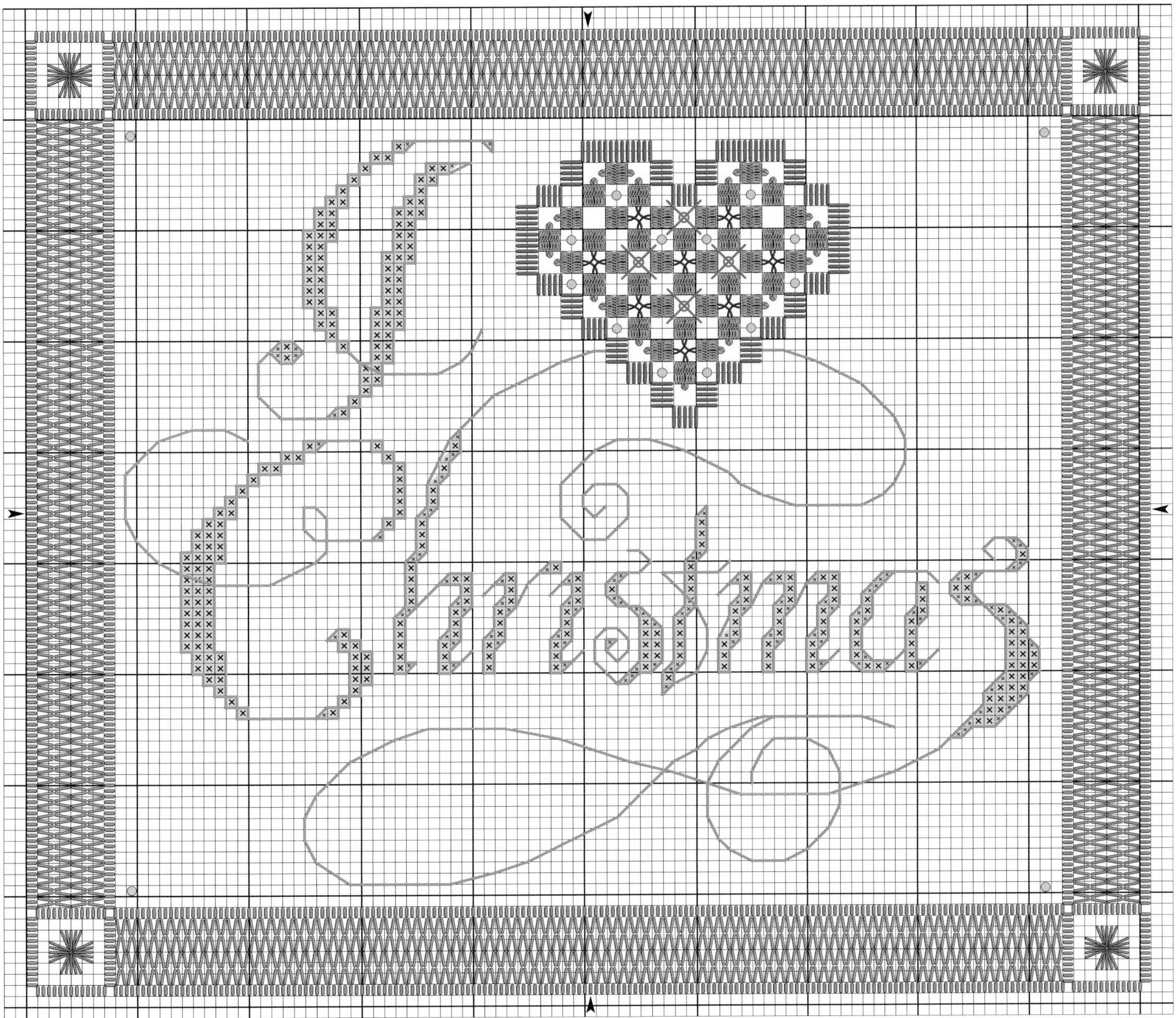

I Love Christmas Key

Anchor DMC
212 ☒ 561 Seafoam

BACKSTITCH
212 ／ 561 Seafoam – letter outline (1X), lettering swirls (2X)

SATIN STITCH
387 Ecru – border (3X)
Ecru #5 pearl cotton – heart Kloster blocks

CROSS EYELET
Ecru #12 pearl cotton – corners

WAVE-FILLING STITCH
Ecru #12 pearl cotton – border

NEEDLEWEAVING WITH PICOT
Ecru #12 pearl cotton – heart

NEEDLEWEAVING WITH DOVE'S EYE
Ecru #12 pearl cotton – heart

NEEDLEWEAVING WITH WEB
Ecru #12 pearl cotton – heart

MILL HILL BEADS
03021 Royal pearl seed beads

Stitch count: *87 high x 101 wide*
Finished design size:
25-count fabric – 7 x 8 inches

Come Home to Christmas

Glue a star to the top of each tree. Trim ⅛" from each edge of the felt triangles. Center and glue the felt triangles to the backs of the trees. Use a darning needle or metal skewer to make a hole through the fabric and into the foam-core board at the bottom center of the tree. Cut three lengths of ⅛-diameter dowel, measuring from 6" to 9". Insert and glue one end of a dowel length into each hole.

Favorite Things

Materials

36-count cream Edinburgh linen: 10×11" piece for large tree, 9×10" piece for medium tree, and 8×9" piece for small tree
Cotton embroidery floss
Kreinik blending filament
Mill Hill petite seed beads
Tracing paper
Foam core board
Fleece
Cream felt
Thick white crafts glue
Mill Hill Glass Treasures: Star #12166
⅛"-diameter wooden dowel
Large darning needle or metal skewer

Instructions

For the large tree, find the center of a short edge of the 10×11" piece of linen. Measure down 3" and begin stitching the top center of the Favorite Things chart *opposite* there. Stitch the entire design in rows from top to bottom, completing each row before moving to the next. For the medium tree, begin stitching the top center of the tree 3" below the center of a 9" edge; stitch the chart from top to bottom, eliminating the last two rows. For the small tree, begin stitching the top center of the tree 3" below the center of an 8" edge; stitch the chart from top to bottom, eliminating the last five rows. Use two plies of floss to work the stitches over two threads of the fabric unless otherwise specified. Attach the beads with one ply of floss. Press the stitched pieces from the back.

Place tracing paper over each stitched piece and draw a triangle outline ½" beyond the outermost stitches. Cut out the paper patterns on the traced line. Draw around each pattern one time onto the foam-core board and cut out. Use the patterns to cut a matching shape from both the fleece and the felt.

Center and glue a fleece triangle on one side of the corresponding foam-core triangles. Center the fleece side of the foam-core board on the back of the corresponding stitched piece. Trim the fabric ½" beyond the edges of the board. Fold the fabric to the back; glue in place.

Favorite Things Key

ANCHOR DMC

CROSS-STITCH (2X)
1025 347 Deep salmon
877 502 Medium blue-green
876 503 True blue-green
889 610 Deep drab brown
1024 3328 Dark salmon

BLENDED NEEDLE CROSS-STITCH
306 729 Old gold (1X) and 002 Kreinik gold blending filament (1X)

BACKSTITCH (1X)
879 501 Dark blue-green – green stems and lettering
889 610 Deep drab brown – all other stitches

BLENDED NEEDLE BACKSTITCH
306 729 Old gold (1X) and Kreinik gold blending filament (1X)

ALGERIAN EYELET (1X over 4 threads)
306 729 Old gold (1X) and 002 Kreinik gold blending filament (1X)

FRENCH KNOT (1X wrapped twice)
1025 347 Deep salmon – holly berries
879 501 Dark blue-green – lettering

SATIN STITCH (1X)
876 503 True blue-green

MILL HILL PETITE GLASS SEED BEAD
40557 Gold

Stitch count: *91 high x 71 wide*

Finished design size:
36-count fabric – 5 x 4 inches

Favorite Things

Nordic Stocking Ornaments

Materials

For each ornament:
8×10" piece of 16-count antique white, dark blue, Victorian red, or tartan green Aida cloth
Cotton embroidery floss
5×7" piece of fusible interfacing
Erasable fabric marker
6×8" piece of cotton fabric to match Aida cloth
⅝ yard of purchased red, blue, green or white sew-in piping
Matching sewing thread
6" length of ¼"-wide satin ribbon (optional)

Instructions

Center and stitch the Nordic Stocking Ornaments chart *opposite* on the Aida cloth. Use two plies of floss from the desired color option to work the stitches over one square of the fabric unless otherwise specified. Press from the back.

Center and fuse the interfacing to the back of the stitched piece, following the manufacturer's instructions. Use an erasable fabric marker to draw the stocking outline as indicated by the dashed line on the chart. Cut out the stocking shape ½" beyond the marked outline. Use the stocking as a pattern to cut a matching back from the cotton fabric. For the hanger, cut a 1×6" hanging strip from the remaining cotton fabric.

With raw edges even and using a zipper foot, baste the piping around the sides and foot of the stocking front. With right sides together, sew the stocking front to the back along the basting lines, leaving the top edge open. Trim the seams and clip the curves. Turn the stocking right side out; press.

For a fabric hanger, press under ¼" along each long edge of the 1×6" hanging strip. Fold the strip in half lengthwise, aligning pressed edges; press again. Sew the long edges together opposite the fold. Fold the strip in half to form a loop. Baste the ends to the top outer corner on the heel side of the stocking. For a ribbon hanger, fold the ribbon in half and baste the ends to the top outer corner. Baste piping around the top edge of the stocking, raw edges even. Press the seam allowances into the stocking.

Toile Sampler

Materials

16×14" piece of 18-count pussy willow gray Aida cloth
Cotton embroidery floss
Desired frame

Instructions

Center and stitch the Toile Sampler chart on *pages 108–109* on the fabric. Use two plies of floss to work the stitches over one square of the fabric unless otherwise specified. Press the stitched piece from the back. Frame the piece as desired.

Reindeer Gift Tags

Materials

8" square of 18-count pussy willow gray Aida cloth
Cotton embroidery floss
Three coordinating sheets of paper
Glue stick
¼" hole punch
Self-adhesive ½"-diameter foam circles
22" length of ¾"-wide sheer ribbon

Instructions

Center and stitch the reindeer motif from the Toile Sampler chart on *pages 108–109* onto the Aida cloth. Use two plies of Dark pistachio (DMC 319) or Light garnet (DMC 816) to work the cross-stitches over one square of fabric. Press the stitched piece from the back.

Centering the design, trim the stitched piece into a $2\frac{3}{4}\times3\frac{3}{4}$" rectangle. From the coordinating papers, cut one 3×4" rectangle, one $3\frac{1}{2}\times4\frac{1}{2}$" rectangle, and one $3\frac{3}{4}\times4\frac{3}{4}$" rectangle. Cut a $1\frac{3}{4}\times2\frac{3}{4}$" opening centered in the small rectangle, creating a frame.

Mount the medium rectangle on the large rectangle with the glue stick. Use the hole punch to make two holes $\frac{1}{2}$" apart, centering them $\frac{1}{4}$" from one short edge of the layered rectangles. Center and mount the stitched piece on the medium rectangle with the glue stick. Center and mount the frame on the stitched piece with adhesive foam circles. Thread the ribbon through the holes and tie to the package.

Nordic Stocking Ornaments

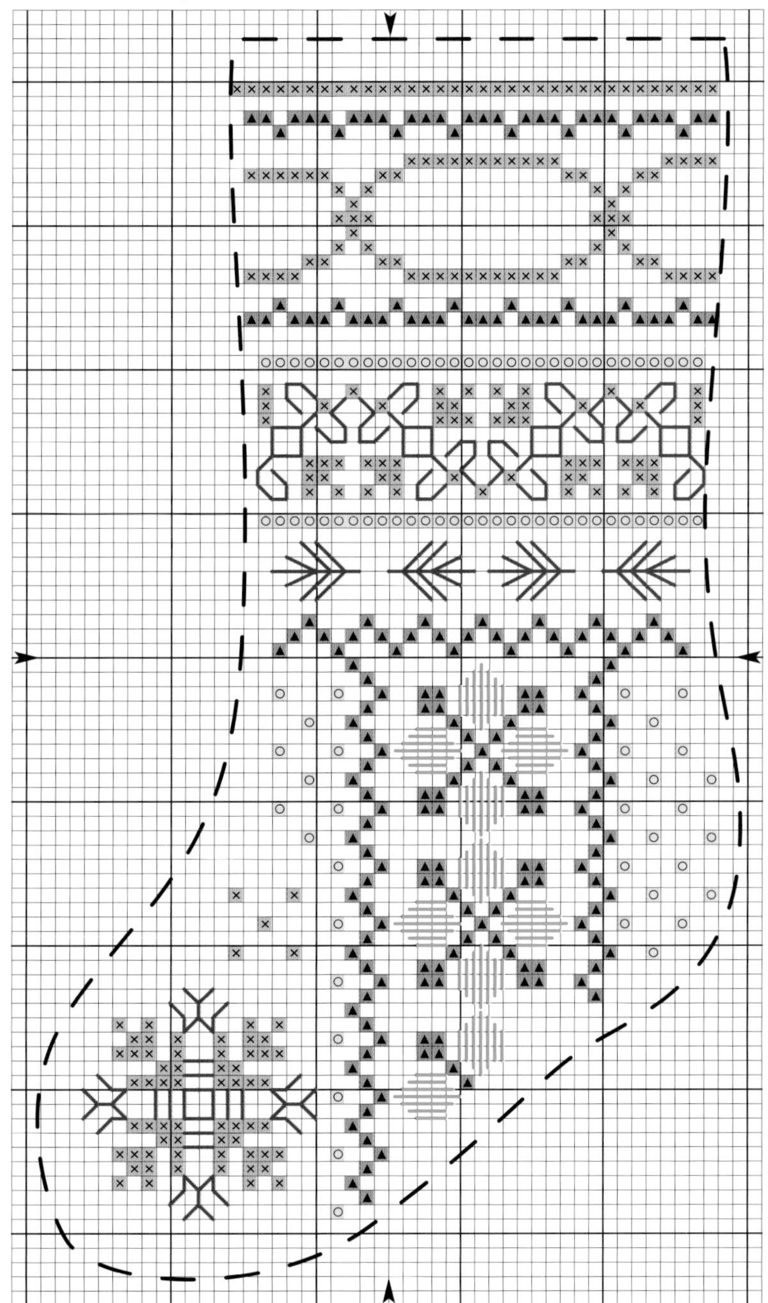

Nordic Stocking Ornaments Key

BLUE OPTION

ANCHOR DMC

CROSS-STITCH (2X)

133 ▲ 796 Royal blue
137 ⊠ 798 Delft blue
148 ◎ 803 Baby blue

BACKSTITCH (1X)

133 / 796 Royal blue – all stitches

SATIN STITCH (2X)

137 798 Delft blue – flowers

GREEN OPTION

ANCHOR DMC

CROSS-STITCH (2X)

210 ▲ 562 Medium seafoam
204 ⊠ 563 True seafoam
206 ◎ 564 Light seafoam

BACKSTITCH (1X)

210 / 562 Medium seafoam – all stitches

SATIN STITCH (2X)

204 563 True seafoam – flowers

RED OPTION

ANCHOR DMC

CROSS-STITCH (2X)

045 ▲ 814 Dark garnet
044 ⊠ 815 Medium garnet
019 ◎ 304 Christmas red

BACKSTITCH (1X)

045 / 814 Dark garnet – all stitches

SATIN STITCH (2X)

044 815 Medium garnet – flowers

Stitch count: *86 high x 49 wide*

Finished design sizes:
16-count fabric – $5\frac{3}{8}$ x 3 inches

Come Home to Christmas

Toile Sampler Key

ANCHOR DMC

CROSS-STITCH (2X)

979 ▲ 312 Medium navy

977 ☒ 334 Light navy

129 ⊡ 3325 Pale navy

Stitch count: *184 high x 135 wide*

Finished design size:
18-count fabric – $10\frac{1}{4}$ x $7\frac{1}{2}$ inches

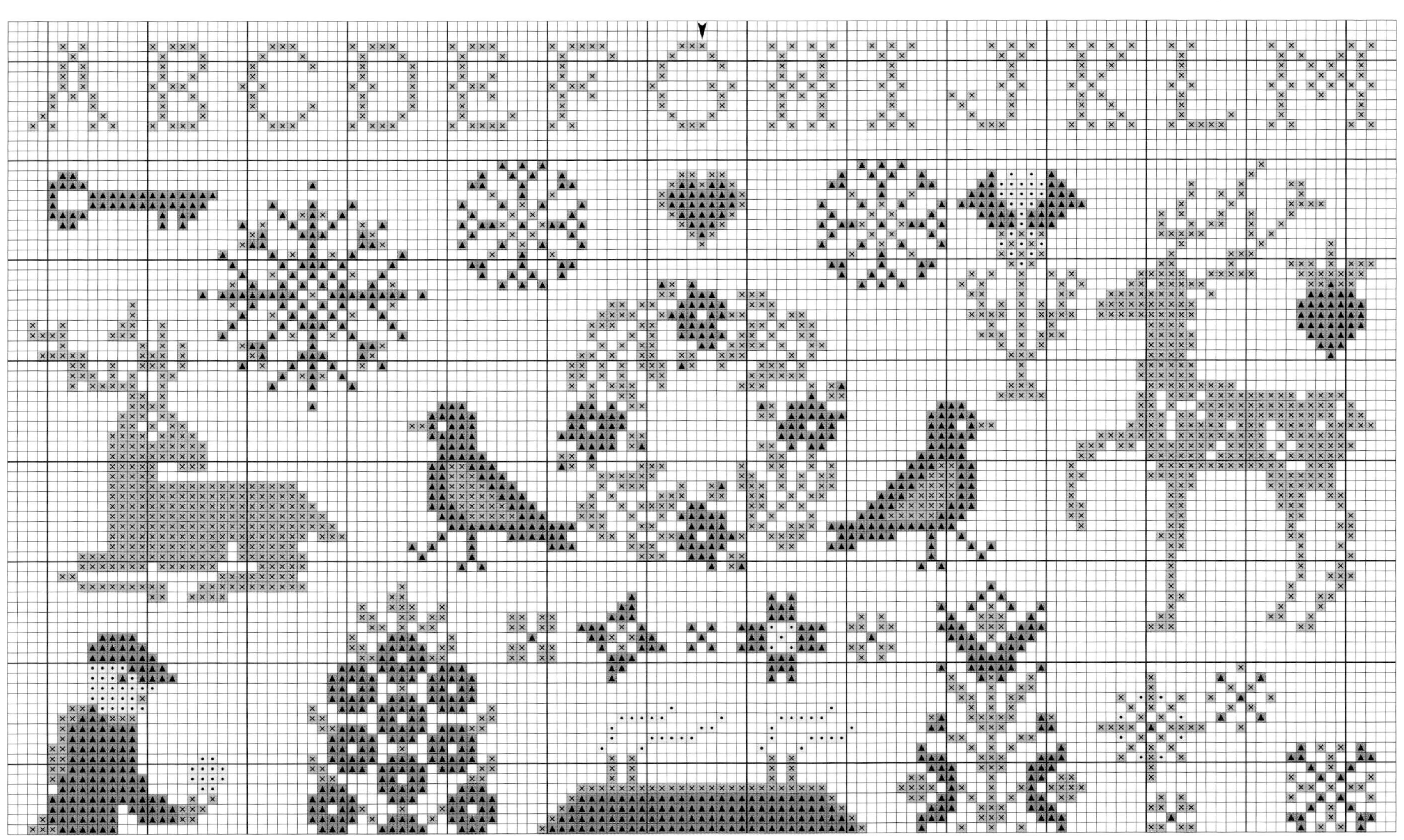

Believe Angel

Materials

For each ornament or framed piece:

9×12" piece of 32-count antique white Lugana fabric
Cotton embroidery floss
5x9" piece of coordinating cotton fabric
7" length of ¼"-wide ribbon
Matching sewing thread
Polyester fiberfill
Two ¼"-diameter pink heart buttons
Heirloom acid-free glue

Instructions

Center and stitch the Believe Angel chart on *page 114* onto the fabric. Use two plies of floss to work the stitches over two threads of the fabric unless otherwise specified. Press the stitched piece from the back. Attach the buttons using two plies of matching floss. Frame the piece as desired.

To make an ornament, trim the stitched piece ¾" beyond the stitched area, rounding the top corners. Use the trimmed stitched piece as a pattern to cut a matching back from the coordinating fabric. Fold the ribbon in half to make a hanging loop. Sew the ribbon ends to the top center of the stitched piece.

With right sides facing, sew the ornament front to the back with a ¼" seam allowance, leaving an opening along the bottom for turning and stuffing. Trim the corners. Turn the ornament right side out and press. Stuff the ornament with polyester fiberfill. Slip-stitch the opening closed. Attach the buttons with acid-free glue.

Rag Bag Santa

Materials

9×12" piece of 32-count raw Belfast linen
Cotton embroidery floss
Four assorted ⅜"-diameter buttons
5×9" piece of coordinating cotton fabric
Three 7" lengths of raffia ribbon
Matching sewing thread
Polyester fiberfill
1"-wide plaid bow

Instructions

Center and stitch the Rag Bag Santa chart on *page 115* on the fabric. Use two plies of floss to work the stitches over two threads of the fabric unless otherwise specified. Press the stitched piece from the back. Attach the buttons using two plies of matching floss. Frame the piece as desired.

To make an ornament, trim the stitched piece ¾" beyond the outermost stitches, rounding the top corners. Use the trimmed stitched piece as a pattern to cut a matching back from the coordinating fabric. For the hanging loop, fold the lengths of raffia ribbon in half. Sew the ribbon ends to the center top of the stitched piece.

With right sides facing, sew the front and back ornament pieces together using a ¼" seam allowance, and leaving an opening along the bottom for turning and stuffing. Trim the corners. Turn the ornament right side out and press. Stuff the ornament with polyester fiberfill. Slip-stitch the opening closed. Attach the bow with matching floss.

Americana Santa Stocking

Materials

14×19" piece of 16-count antique white Aida cloth
Cotton embroidery floss
Erasable fabric marker
10×15" piece of fusible fleece
½ yard of red cotton fabric
1½ yard of purchased red sew-in piping
Matching sewing thread

Instructions

Find the center of the Aida cloth and the center of the Americana Santa Stocking chart on *pages 112–113.* Begin stitching there. Use two plies of floss to work the stitches over one square of the fabric unless otherwise specified. Press the stitched piece from the back.

Center and fuse the fleece to the back of the stitched piece, following the manufacturer's instructions. Use the

erasable fabric marker to draw the stocking outline as indicated by the dashed line on the chart. Cut out the stocking shape ½" beyond the marked outline.

Use the trimmed stitched piece as a pattern to cut a matching back and two lining pieces from the red fabric. From the remaining red fabric, cut a 1½×5" hanging strip.

With raw edges even and using a zipper foot, baste the piping around the sides and foot of the stocking front. Sew the stocking front to the back, right sides together, along the basting lines, leaving the top edge open. Trim the seams and clip the curves. Turn the stocking right side out; press.

For the hanger, press under ⅜" along each long edge of the 1½×5" hanging strip. Fold the strip in half lengthwise, aligning pressed edges; press again. Sew the long edges together opposite the fold. Fold the strip in half to form a loop. Baste the ends to the top outer corner on the heel side of the stocking. Baste piping around the top edge of the stocking with raw edges even.

With right sides facing, sew the lining pieces together with a ½" seam allowance, leaving the top edge open and an opening on one side for turning. Trim the seams and clip the curves; do not turn. Slip the stocking inside the lining, right sides together. Sew the top edges of the stocking and lining together; turn right side out. Slip-stitch the opening closed. Tuck the lining into the stocking; press.

Americana Santa Figure

Materials

- 10×12" piece of 14-count white Aida cloth
- Cotton embroidery floss
- 9×10" piece of fusible fleece
- Erasable fabric marker
- ¼ yard of red cotton fabric
- Matching sewing thread
- 1 yard of purchased red sew-in narrow piping
- 4×6" piece of tracing paper
- Polyester fiberfill
- Plastic pellets
- Sandwich bag and twist tie

Instructions

Center and stitch the Santa from the Americana Santa Stocking chart on *pages 112–113* on the Aida cloth. Use three plies of floss to work the cross-stitches over one square of the fabric. Backstitch with one ply of floss. Press the stitched piece from the back.

Center and fuse the fleece to the back of the stitched piece, following the manufacturer's instructions. Referring to the photograph *opposite,* use the erasable fabric marker to draw an outline about ¾" beyond the outermost stitches, simplifying the shape, keeping the curves smooth, and making a straight line across the bottom edge. Cut out the shape ½" beyond the drawn line. Use the stitched piece as a pattern to cut a matching back from the red cotton fabric.

With raw edges even and using a zipper foot, baste the piping around the top and sides of the stitched piece. With right sides together, sew the stitched piece to the back along the basting line, leaving the bottom edge open. Trim the seams and clip the curves.

Fold the tracing paper in quarters. Align the folds with the dashed lines on the base pattern on *page 125* and trace. Cut out the pattern. Use the fabric marker to draw around the pattern on the red fabric. Cut out ½" beyond the drawn lines.

Baste piping around the bottom edge of the figure. With right sides facing, sew the base fabric to the open edges of the figure along the basting line, leaving an opening for turning and stuffing. Turn the figure right side out.

Stuff the figure firmly with polyester fiberfill, leaving the bottom 2" unstuffed. Fill a sandwich bag with plastic pellets; seal. Insert the bag into the bottom of the figure. Add fiberfill around the bag until the figure is firm. Slip-stitch the opening closed.

Americana Santa Stocking Alphabet Chart

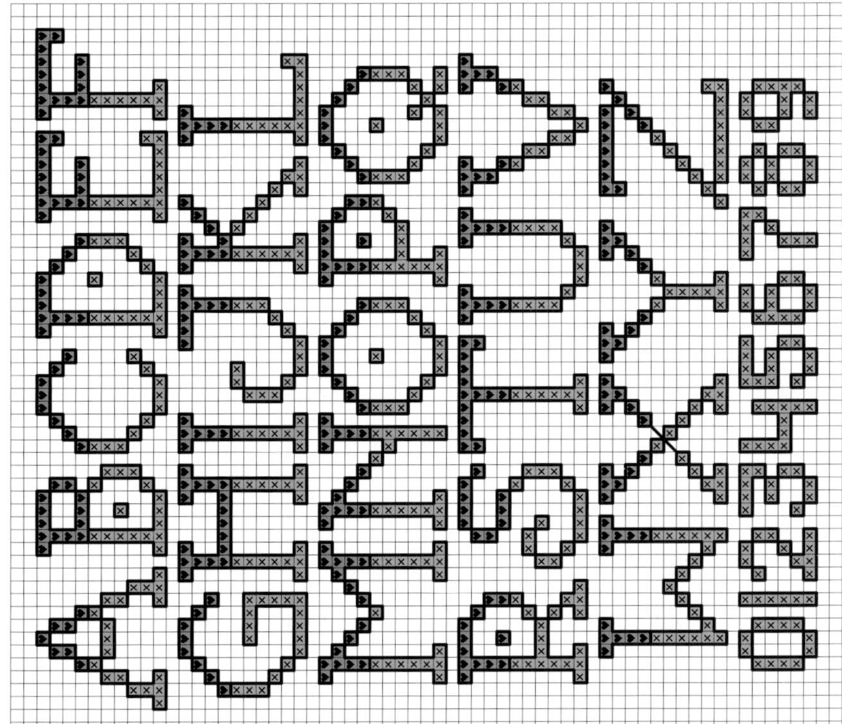

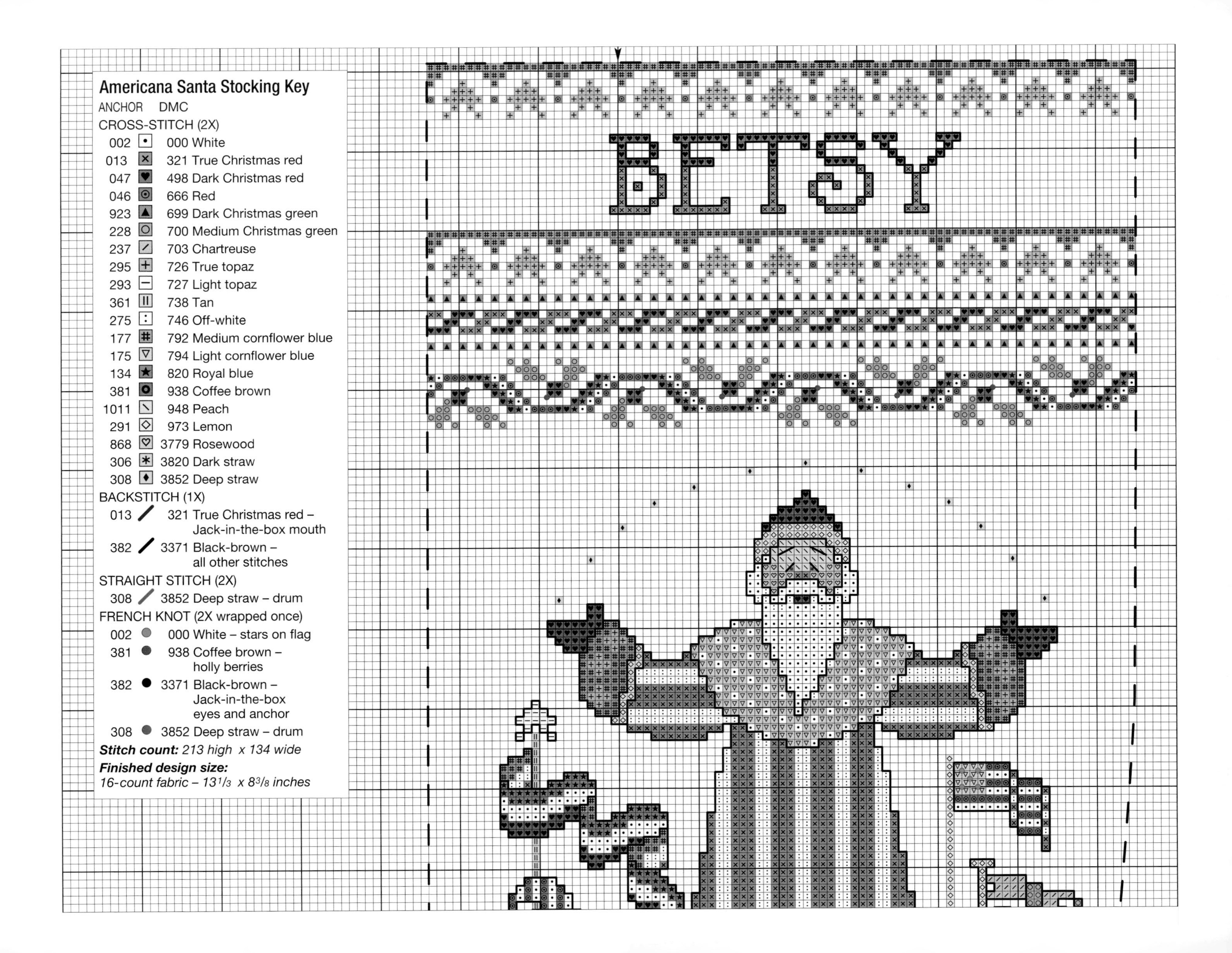

Americana Santa Stocking Key
ANCHOR DMC
CROSS-STITCH (2X)
002 000 White
013 321 True Christmas red
047 498 Dark Christmas red
046 666 Red
923 699 Dark Christmas green
228 700 Medium Christmas green
237 703 Chartreuse
295 726 True topaz
293 727 Light topaz
361 738 Tan
275 746 Off-white
177 792 Medium cornflower blue
175 794 Light cornflower blue
134 820 Royal blue
381 938 Coffee brown
1011 948 Peach
291 973 Lemon
868 3779 Rosewood
306 3820 Dark straw
308 3852 Deep straw
BACKSTITCH (1X)
013 321 True Christmas red – Jack-in-the-box mouth
382 3371 Black-brown – all other stitches
STRAIGHT STITCH (2X)
308 3852 Deep straw – drum
FRENCH KNOT (2X wrapped once)
002 000 White – stars on flag
381 938 Coffee brown – holly berries
382 3371 Black-brown – Jack-in-the-box eyes and anchor
308 3852 Deep straw – drum
Stitch count: 213 high x 134 wide
Finished design size:
16-count fabric – 13 1/3 x 8 3/8 inches
BETSY

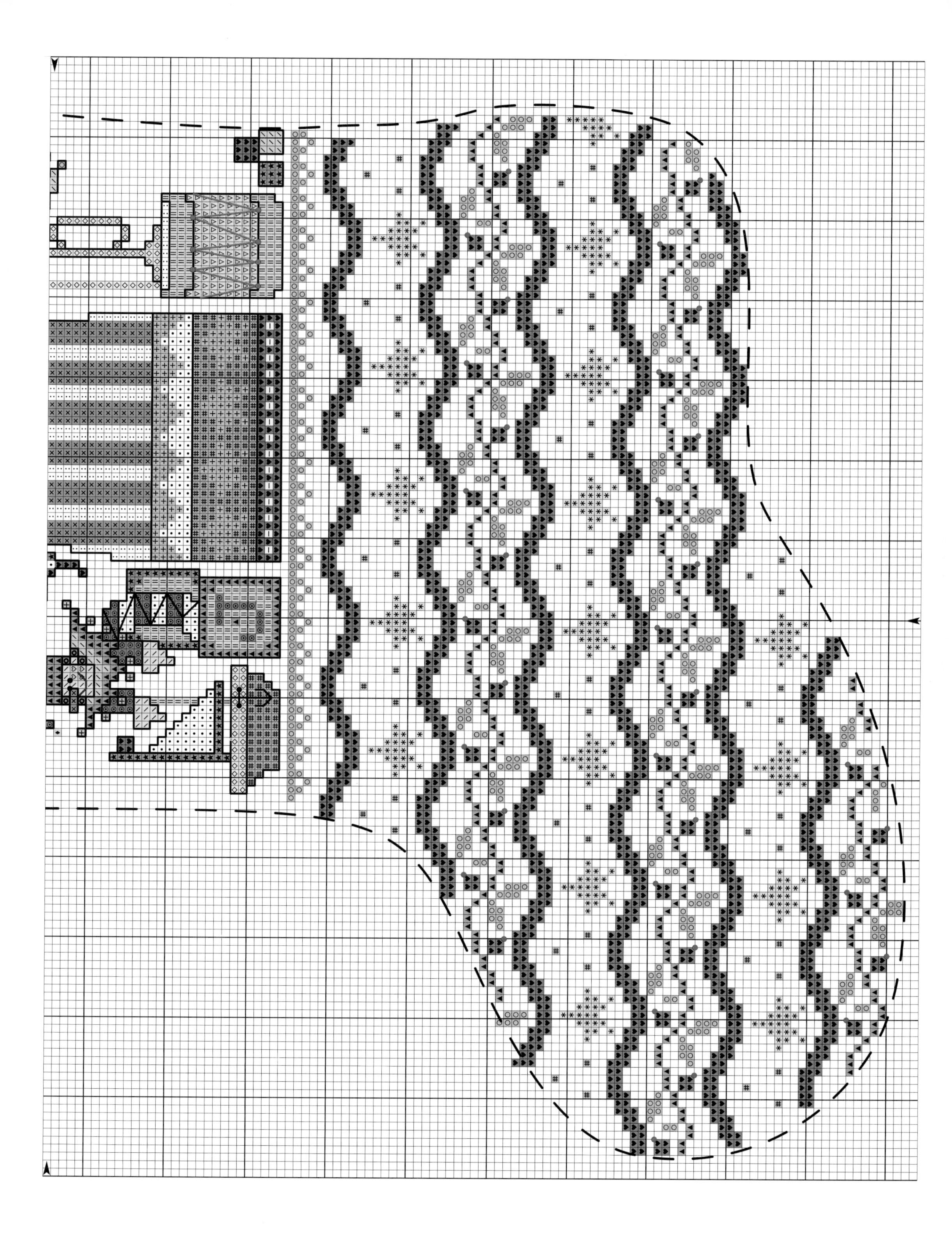

Believe Angel

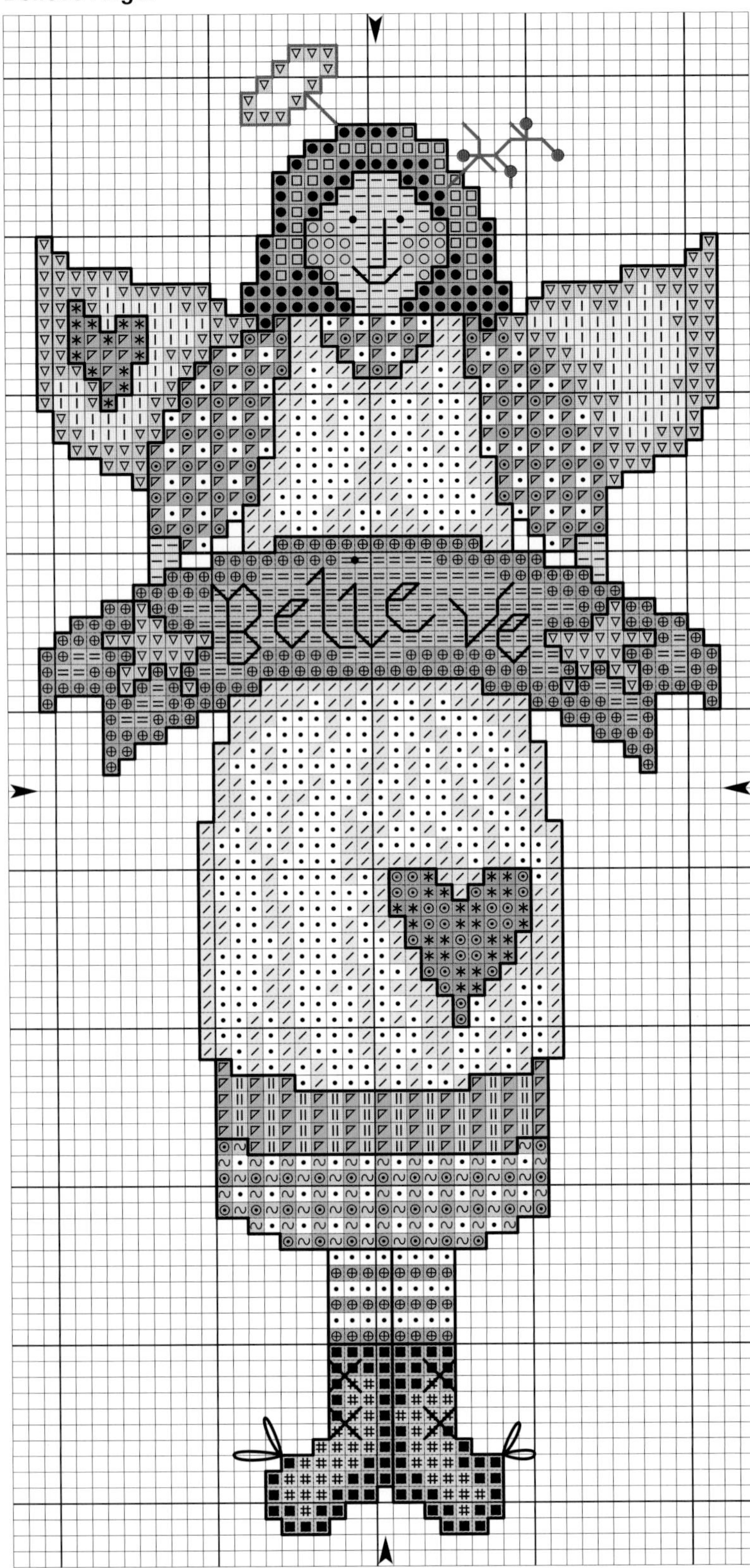

Believe Angel Key

ANCHOR DMC

CROSS-STITCH (2X)

ANCHOR	DMC
002	000 White
895	223 Medium shell pink
892	225 Pale shell pink
399	318 LIght steel
235	414 Dark steel
374	420 Medium hazel
877	502 Medium blue-green
874	676 Light old gold
885	677 Pale old gold
838	926 True slate green
837	927 Light slate green
397	3072 Beaver gray
1027	3722 True shell pink
882	3773 Medium rose-beige
880	3774 Pale rose-beige
875	3813 Light blue-green
373	3828 True hazel

BACKSTITCH (1X)

ANCHOR	DMC
879	501 Dark blue-green – holly spray
306	729 Medium old gold – halo
236	3799 Charcoal – all other stitches

STRAIGHT STITCH (1X)

ANCHOR	DMC
236	3799 Charcoal – shoelaces

FRENCH KNOT (1X wrapped twice)

ANCHOR	DMC
896	3721 Dark shell pink – holly berries
236	3799 Charcoal – eyes, dot on "i"

LAZY DAISY (2X)

ANCHOR	DMC
236	3799 Charcoal – shoelaces

Stitch count: *94 high x 43 wide*

Finished design size:
32-count fabric – 5 7/8 x 2 5/8 inches

Rag Bag Santa

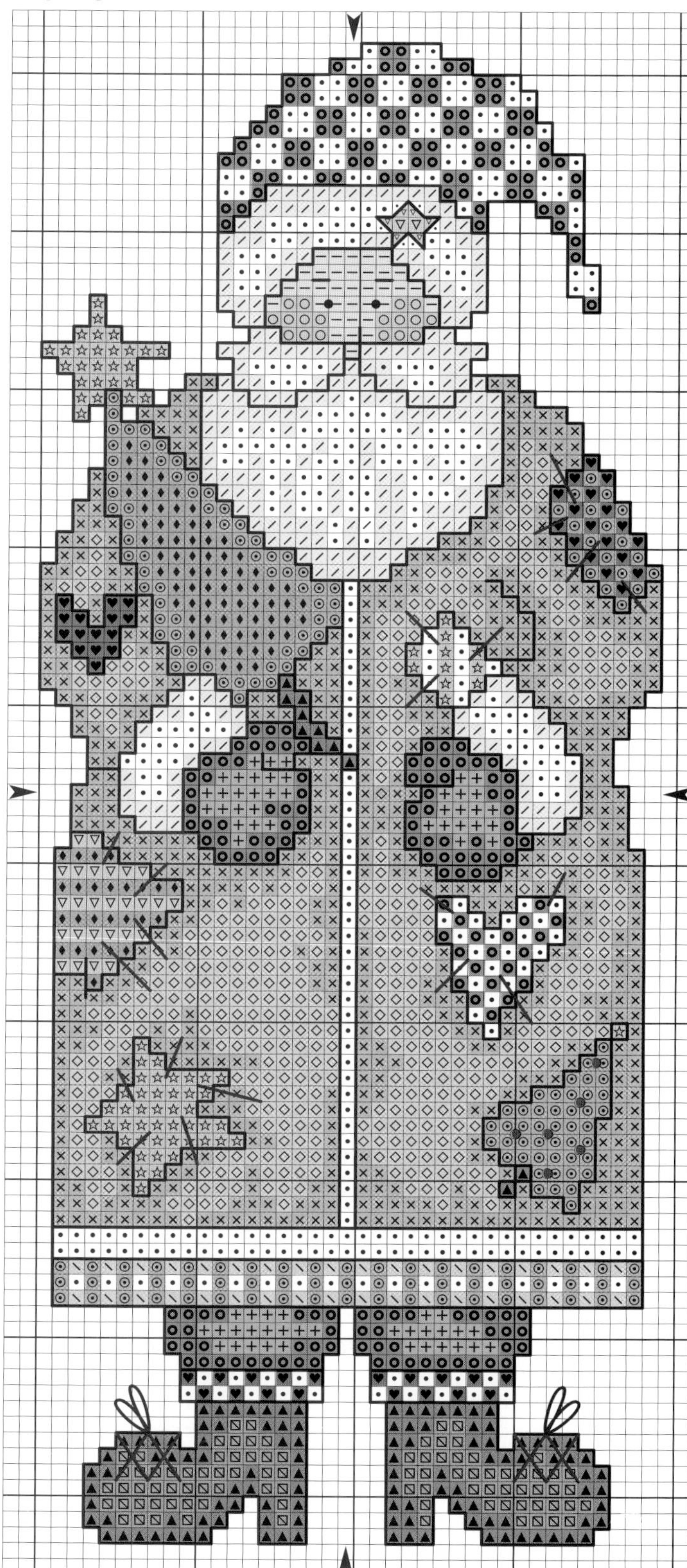

Rag Bag Santa Key

ANCHOR DMC

CROSS-STITCH (2X)

ANCHOR	DMC
002	000 White
1025	347 Deep salmon
879	501 Dark blue-green
877	502 Medium blue-green
1042	504 Pale blue-green
874	676 Light old gold
306	729 Medium old gold
1034	931 Medium antique blue
1033	932 Light antique blue
397	3072 Beaver gray
1024	3328 Dark salmon
1023	3712 Medium salmon
882	3773 Medium rose-beige
880	3774 Pale rose-beige
944	3862 Dark mocha-beige
379	3863 Medium mocha-beige

BACKSTITCH (1X)

236 3799 Charcoal – all stitches

STRAIGHT STITCH (1X)

236 3799 Charcoal – shoelaces, patches

FRENCH KNOT (1X wrapped twice)

1025 347 Deep salmon – Christmas tree on coat

236 3799 Charcoal – eyes

LAZY DAISY (2X)

236 3799 Charcoal – shoelaces

Stitch count: *95 high x 39 wide*

Finished design size:
32-count fabric – 6 x 2 1/2 inches

Come Home to Christmas

Cross-Stitch Basics

Getting Started

The written instructions for each project indicate where to begin stitching. For most projects the starting point is at the center. Every chart has arrows that indicate the horizontal and vertical centers. With your finger, trace along the grid to the point where the two centers meet. Compare a symbol at the center of the chart to the key and choose which floss color to stitch first. To find the center of the fabric, fold it into quarters and finger-crease or baste along the folds with a single ply of contrasting floss.

Cut the floss into 15" lengths, and separate all six plies. Recombine the plies as indicated in the project instructions, and thread them into a blunt-tip needle.

Basic Cross-Stitch

Make one cross-stitch for each symbol on the chart. For horizontal rows, stitch the first diagonal of each stitch in the row. Work back across the row, completing each stitch. On most linen and even-weave fabrics, work the stitches over two threads as shown in the diagram at *right.* On Aida cloth, each stitch should cover one square.

You also can work cross-stitches in the reverse direction. Remember to embroider the stitches uniformly—that is, always work the top half of each stitch in the same direction.

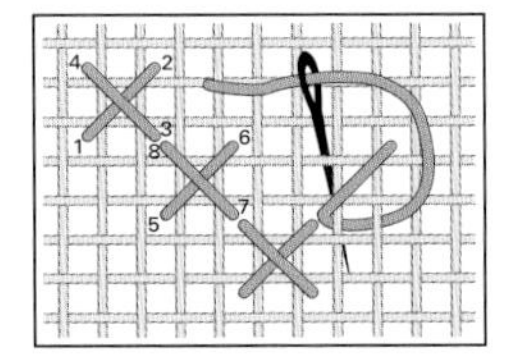

Cross-stitch worked singly

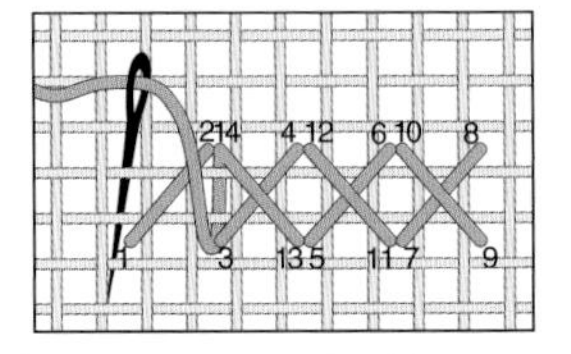

Cross-stitch worked in rows

To secure thread at the beginning

The most common way to secure the beginning tail of the thread is to hold it under the first four or five stitches.

To secure the thread with a waste knot,

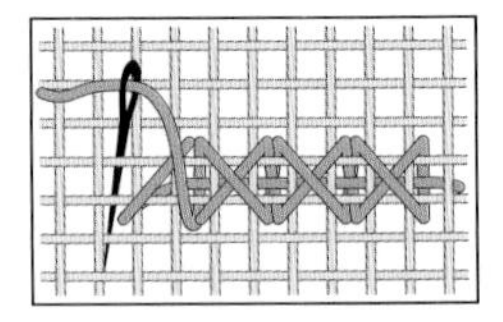

Stitching over the thread tail

thread the needle and knot the end of the thread. Insert the needle from the right side of fabric, about 4 inches away from the first stitch. Bring the needle up through the fabric, and work the first series of stitches. When finished, clip the knot on the right side. Rethread the needle with excess floss and push the needle through to the stitches on the wrong side of the fabric.

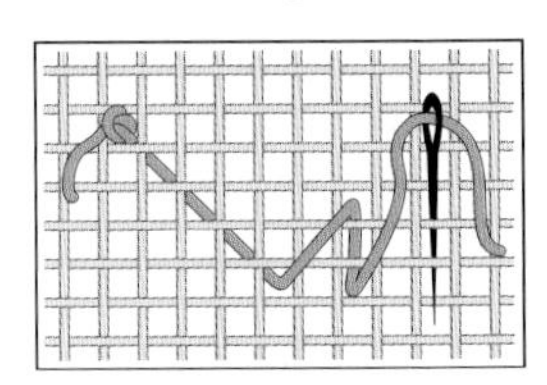

Waste knot

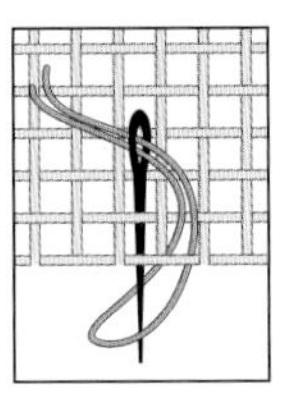

Loop knot

When working with two, four, or six plies of floss, use a loop knot. Cut half as many plies of thread, making each one twice as long. Recombine the plies, fold the strand in half, and thread all of the ends into the needle. Work the first diagonal of the first stitch, and before pulling the thread all the way through, slip the needle through the loop formed by folding the thread.

To secure thread at the end

To finish, slip the threaded needle under previously stitched threads on the wrong side of the fabric for four or five stitches, weaving the thread back and forth a few times. Clip the thread.

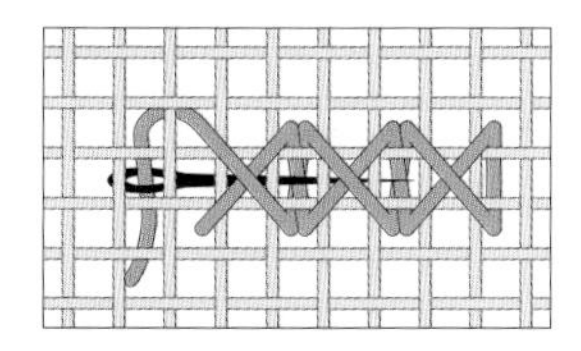

Securing thread at the end

Smyrna Cross-Stitch

A Smyrna cross-stitch consists of an X-shape stitch topped by a straight horizontal stitch and a straight vertical stitch. It's often worked over four, six, eight, or more threads.

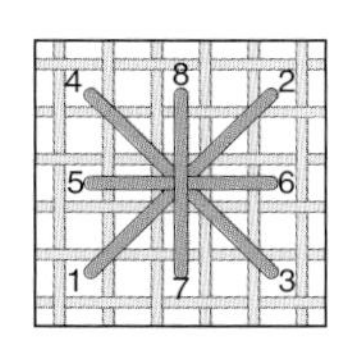

Smyrna cross-stitch

Quarter and Three-Quarter Cross-Stitches

To obtain rounded shapes in a design, use quarter and three-quarter cross-stitches. On linen and even-weave fabrics, a quarter cross-stitch will extend from the corner to the center intersection of threads. To make quarter cross-stitches on Aida cloth, estimate the center of the square. Three-quarter

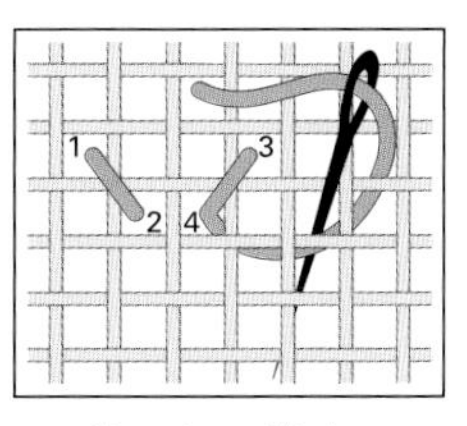

Quarter stitches

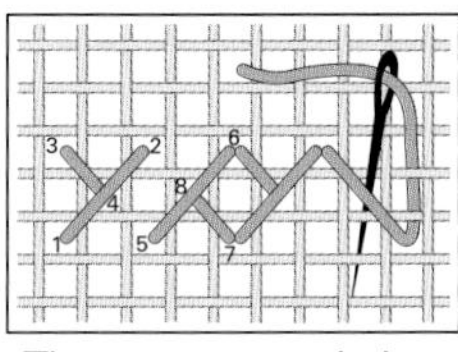

Three-quarter stitches

cross-stitches combine a quarter cross-stitch with a half cross-stitch. Both stitches may slant in any direction.

Backstitches

Backstitches define and outline the shapes of a design. For most projects, backstitches require only one ply of floss. On the color key, (2X) indicates two plies of floss, (3X) indicates three plies, etc.

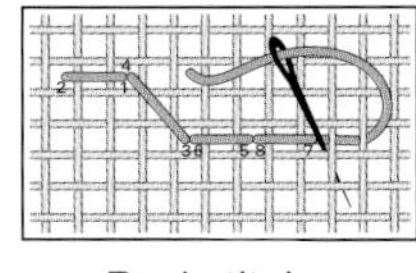

Backstitches

Couching

Use two needles to work a line of couching. Bring the heavier couched thread through the fabric at the beginning of the line designated on the chart and to the back at the end. Roughly align it in the position

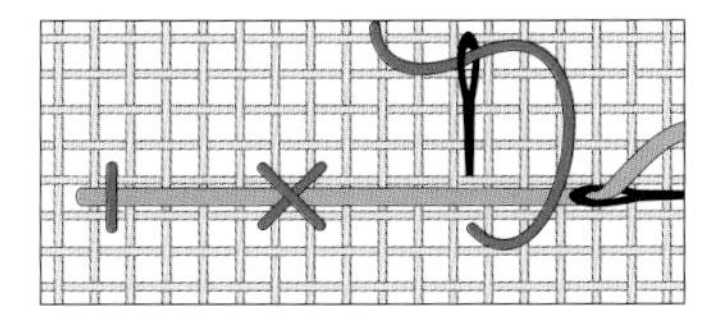

Couching

indicated on the chart. Bring the lighter couching thread through the fabric four threads (unless otherwise specified on chart) beyond the entry point of the couched thread, over it, and to the back in the next hole. Move four threads along the line of the couched thread, and repeat the couching. Continue along the entire length of the couched thread.

Algerian Eyelet

The key to making this spoked stitch with its center hole is to work from the outside in. Bring the needle from the back to the front at an outside edge of the stitch; then push it to the back at the midpoint of the stitch, pulling the thread firmly and gently. As you work successive spokes, an opening will appear in the middle.

Algerian eyelets in a row

Chain Stitch

Bring the needle to the front of the fabric, and return to the back through the same hole, forming a loop. Slide the tip of the needle under two or more threads and bring it to the front of the fabric. Slip the loop under the needle tip. Pull gently until the loop lies smoothly on the fabric. Pass the needle to the back, forming the loop of the second stitch of the chain.

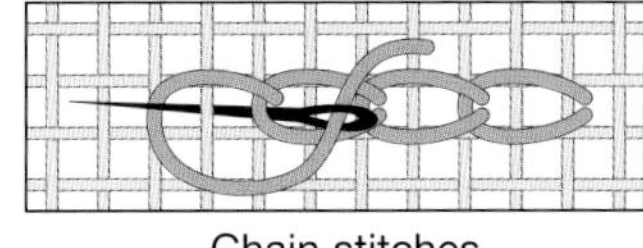

Chain stitches

Cross-Stitch Basics

Cross-Stitches with Beads

Beads may be attached by working the first half of each cross-stitch and attaching a bead on the return stitch. To ensure that beads stand up straight, work with two plies of floss and add the bead to the first half stitch. As you work the second diagonal, split the plies so one ply lies on each side of the bead.

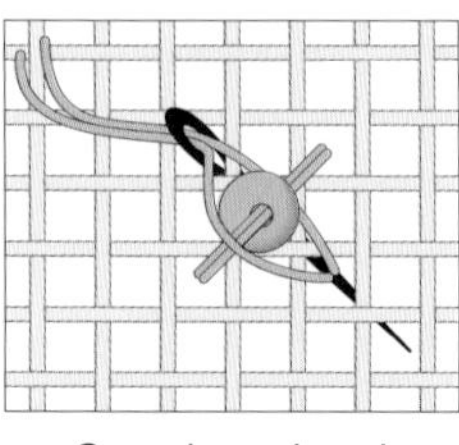

Securing a bead

Lazy-Daisy Stitch

Bring the needle to the front of the fabric, and return to the back through the same hole, forming a loop. Slide the tip of the needle under two or more threads; then bring it to the front of the fabric. Slip the loop under the needle tip. Pull gently until the loop lies smoothly on the fabric. Push the needle to the back, forming a tack stitch over the end of the loop.

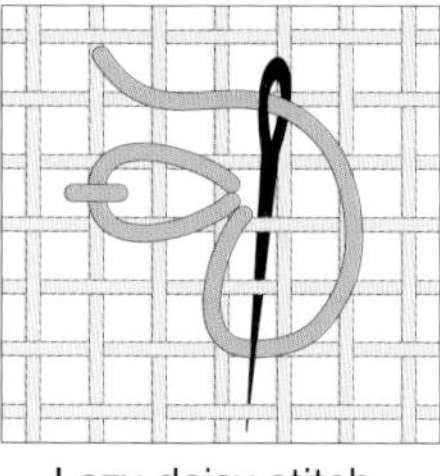

Lazy daisy stitch

French Knot

Bring the threaded needle through the fabric, and wrap the floss around the needle as shown. Tighten the twists, and return the needle through the fabric in the same place. The floss will slide through the wrapped thread to make the knot.

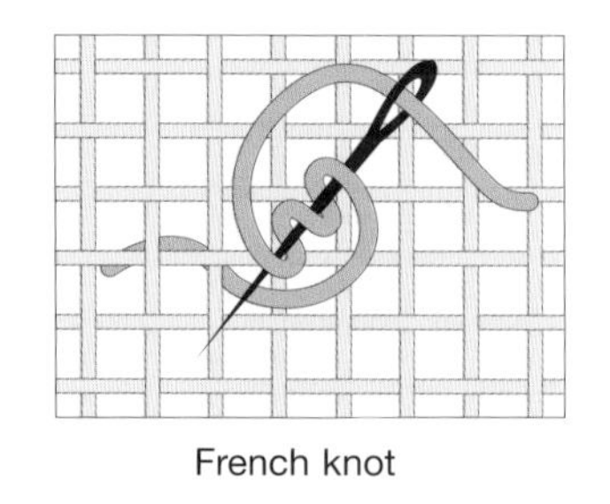

French knot

Half Cross-Stitches

Half cross-stitches are single diagonals. They usually are listed under a separate heading in the color key and are indicated on the chart by a diagonal colored line.

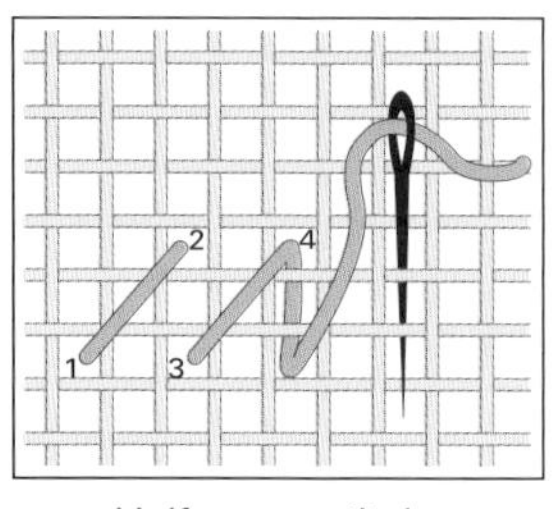

Half cross-stitch

Running Stitch

Running stitches work up fast and add design definition. They are usually equal in length, although uneven stitches create a novelty effect.

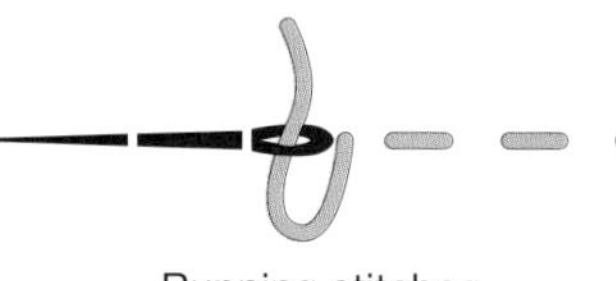

Running stitches

Straight Stitches

Straight stitches, made by simply coming up at one point and going down at another, often are used for sun rays, whiskers, and other simple accents.

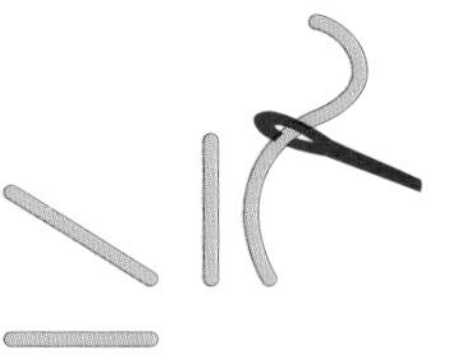

Straight stitches

Satin Stitch

This smooth-surface stitch may be worked over a few or many threads. Bring up the needle up through the first hole. Count threads along a straight line, and return to the back of the fabric. For the second stitch, bring up the needle through the hole immediately next to the first stitch.

Satin stitches

Changing Materials

Many stitchers work cross-stitch designs using fabrics and threads other than those specified in the projects. This information will help you complete the projects in this book while adapting them to your own preferences.

Before you begin a project on a fabric other than that specified, stitch a small sample. Be sure you're happy with the amount of detail on the new fabric, the way the thread covers it, and how the needle slips through the fabric.

Waste Canvas

Aida Cloth

Linen and Evenweave Fabrics

Cross-Stitch Fabrics

Work counted cross-stitch on any fabric that lets you make consistently sized, even stitches. Many fabrics marketed specifically for cross-stitch are interchangeable when the stitch-per-inch counts match. For example, a project that calls for 28-count linen stitched over two threads can easily be worked on 14-count Aida cloth. A higher-count fabric will yield a smaller finished project. When a design is enlarged by working on lower-count fabric, some of the detail may be lost. The charts in this book indicate the size of the design when worked on the recommended fabric.

Aida cloth is the most popular cross-stitch fabric. The threads are woven in groups separated by tiny spaces to create a pattern of squares across the surface of the fabric so a beginning stitcher can easily see where to place the cross-stitches. Measure Aida cloth by the number of squares per inch; for example, 14-count Aida cloth has 14 squares per inch. Look for Aida cloth in 6-, 8-, 11-, 14-, 16-, and 18- thread counts. You'll find 14-count Aida cloth in more than 60 colors. For beginners, white Aida cloth is available with a removable grid of prebasted threads.

Experienced stitchers consider linen to be the standard of excellence in cross-stitch fabrics. The threads used to weave linen vary in thickness, giving the fabric a slightly irregular surface. Measure thread count by the number of threads per inch. Because most designs are worked over two threads, 28-count linen usually yields 14 stitches per inch. Linens are made in counts from 14 (seven stitches per inch) to 45.

The market for specialty fabrics for counted cross-stitch continues to grow with the popularity of the craft. These fabrics are referred to as even-weave fabrics because they're woven from threads with a consistent diameter, although some have a homespun look. Count most even-weaves the way you count linen—by the number of threads per inch—and stitch over two threads.

Use Hardanger fabric for very fine counted cross-stitch. The traditional fabric for Norwegian embroidery of the same name has an over-two, under-two weave that produces 22 small squares per inch.

Use waste canvas to cross-stitch on clothing and fabrics that aren't otherwise suitable for stitching. The canvas marks the squares and is designed to ravel when dampened after stitching is complete. It ranges in count from 6½ to 20 stitches per inch.

Cross-stitch charts also can be worked on 32- or 40-count silk gauze, 14-count perforated paper, 6- to 24-count needlepoint canvas, or plastic canvas. These materials make no provision for fractional (quarter and three-quarter) stitches, so choose a chart with whole stitches only.

Threads for Stitching

Most types of commercially available embroidery thread are adaptable for counted cross-stitch projects.

Six-ply cotton embroidery floss has the widest range of colors, including variegated colors. It separates easily into single or multiple plies for stitching. The instructions with each project in this book list how many plies to use. If you select a different-count

Cross-Stitch Basics

fabric than the one specified, use the chart *below* as a guide, and experiment on a scrap of the fabric until you achieve the desired effect. A greater number of plies will result in a dense or heavily textured piece; a smaller number of plies will create a lightweight or delicate texture.

Fabric	Tapestry Needle Size	# of Plies
11-count	24	3(3x)
14-count	24–26	2(2x)
18-count	26	2(2x)
22-count	26	1(1x)

Rayon and silk floss are similar in weight to six-ply cotton embroidery floss but with a higher sheen. Both can be interchanged with cotton floss, one ply for one ply. Because they have a “slicker” texture, you may find them more difficult to use.

Pearl cotton is available in four sizes: #3, #5, #8, and #12 (#3 is heavy; #12 is fine). It has an obvious twist and a high sheen.

Flower thread is a matte-finish cotton thread. When a design calls for flower thread, substitute two plies of floss for one strand of flower thread.

A product growing in popularity is overdyed thread. Most colors have an irregularly variegated, one-of-a-kind appearance. Cotton floss, silk floss, flower thread, and pearl cotton are all available in this form. All produce a soft, shaded appearance without changing thread colors. The color changes can be enhanced by working each stitch individually.

Specialty threads add a distinctive look to cross-stitch work. They range in weight from hair-fine blending filament, usually used with floss, to ⅛"-wide ribbon. Specialty threads include numerous metallic threads, richly colored and textured threads, and fun-to-stitch glow-in-the-dark threads.

Needle Types

Blunt-tip needles work best on most cross-stitch fabrics because they slide through the holes and between threads without splitting or snagging the fibers. A large-eyed needle accommodates most threads. Some companies sell such needles labeled “cross-stitch,” but they’re identical to tapestry needles—blunt-tipped and large-eyed. Use the chart at *left* to guide you to the right needle size for common fabrics.

An exception to the blunt-tip needle is waste canvas. Since it’s usually basted to a tightly woven fabric, a sharp embroidery needle is required to penetrate the fabric beneath.

Seed beads require very fine needles that will slide through the holes. Two readily available options are a #8 quilting needle, which is short with a tiny eye, and a long beading needle, which has a longer eye.

Calculating Finished Design Sizes

At the end of each cross-stitch key you'll find a finished design size. The dimensions given are for the stitched area of that particular project on the recommended fabric. For example, the Let It Snow design on *page 59* has a finished design size of 6⅞ by 7¼ inches on the key. The stitch count of the design is 96 high by 102 wide. The Let It Snow design was stitched over one square of 14-count Aida cloth.

To calculate the finished design size, divide the number of stitches high and the number wide by the fabric count. For the Let It Snow design, the figures are as follows: 96÷14=6⅞ and 102÷14=7¼.

When a design is stitched on linen or an even-weave fabric, it normally is stitched over two threads. For example, if you’re stitching over two threads on 28-count fabric, you would divide the stitch count by 14 instead of 28.

Knowing how to calculate the finished design sizes opens up your stitching options, allowing you to choose other fabrics than what a project recommends, therefore changing the size of a finished design. The higher the stitch count of the fabric, the smaller the finished piece.

Here is a sample of size changes for a design that is 120 stitches high and 90 stitches wide:

On 14-count fabric, 8½ × 6½ inches
On 18-count fabric, 6⅔ × 5 inches
On 20-count fabric, 6 × 4½ inches

Finish Like a Pro

Getting Started

When all cross-stitches are complete and the last French knots have been made, most pieces still need a frame or some other treatment to make them into useful items.

While some pieces beg to be framed, others are destined to become stockings, ornaments, or pillows, and some aspire to be more novel items such as bellpulls, purses, and bookmarks. Finishing each piece neatly is easy when you know the tricks.

Made for Stitching

Creating a neatly finished project may be as simple as strolling through your favorite needlework store. There are hundreds of no-sewing-required prefinished items you can cross-stitch on. You'll also find a wide variety of easy-to-assemble mounting kits in the form of boxes, trays, paperweights, candle screens, greeting cards, bellpull hardware, drinking cups, napkin rings, flower planters, oversize covered buttons, and purse accessories.

A Sewing Secret

Better Homes and Gardens® crafts editors are often asked how we make our projects look so neat. When it comes to sewing, the answer is baste, baste, baste! While it may seem like a tedious response, when you consider how much time is spent stitching a piece, you'll find the time spent basting is worthwhile to produce a polished finish.

Standard sewing thread can be used for basting, but a single thread of floss is a better choice because it's all cotton and easier to remove. Choose a thread color that contrasts just enough to be seen on the fabric when you stitch by machine; thread that's too dark may leave a color shadow, especially on a light-color fabric. Put away your blunt-tip cross-stitch or tapestry needle and use a sharp needle for basting. Stitches that are ¼ to ½" long will hold layers together when you begin machine stitching.

Trims

Cording, piping, fringe, gathered lace, or ruffles add an attractive finish to a cross-stitched stocking, pillow, or doll. A well-chosen trim enhances the colors of a piece and gives a crisp edge to the project.

Colorful trims abound in the notions and upholstery departments of most fabric stores. Some ropelike trims have a sew-in lip that can be stitched into a seam.

Other trims are simply pretty ropes. They should be hand-sewn to the finished project. These include satin and metallic cords. Another option is to make your own piping or ruffles. Helpful directions for making and applying piping and ruffles begin below.

Piping and Trims

Make Your Own Piping

Depending on the look you want to achieve, you can cover piping with almost any dress-weight fabric. Plain, print, or plaid cotton is an easy-sew choice for a first project. Stiffer and more drapable fabrics such as brocade, velvet, satin, and lamé add elegance. Select fabric that matches the project back or provides a colorful contrast.

If you purchase 44/45"-wide fabric for the back of a stocking, pillow, or doll, and plan to use the same fabric to cover cording, you probably won't need additional fabric to make piping. For contrast piping, purchase ¼ yard of 44/45"-wide fabric. It will make about 80" of piping up to 1" in diameter—more than enough for an 18"-tall stocking or an 18"-square pillow. Purchase more yardage for thicker piping.

While you're fabric shopping, be sure to purchase filler for your piping. To make very narrow piping, you can use cotton string. For thicker piping, look for cotton cording in fabric stores. You'll need the length of the finished piping plus a few inches.

Finish Like a Pro

1. For the designs in this book, we've figured the measurements for every project that includes piping, but if you're designing your own finish, use this geometry formula to determine how wide the piping strips need to be: $C=\pi d$ (circumference equals 3.14 times diameter), and add seam allowances. For example, to cover ½"-diameter cord and leave ¼" seam allowances, strips need to be 2⅛" (3.1 times ½" plus 2 times ¼") wide.

Cut enough strips to equal the length of the filler cord plus about 2" extra per strip (add more for piping thicker than ½" diameter).

Straight-grain piping is easier to sew than bias-cut piping, and works fine for most projects. Cut straight piping strips parallel to the longest edge of the fabric. You'll need to clip the seam allowance at curves and corners to keep them smooth.

Only sharp inside curves such as the inner points of a scalloped edge need bias-covered piping to lie smoothly. However, bias-cut plaid and striped fabrics add interesting texture. If you have quilting tools, use a rotary cutter, mat, and acrylic ruler to cut a 45-degree angle at one end of the fabric. Then cut the strips parallel to the angled line. Or draw angled lines and cut along the lines with scissors.

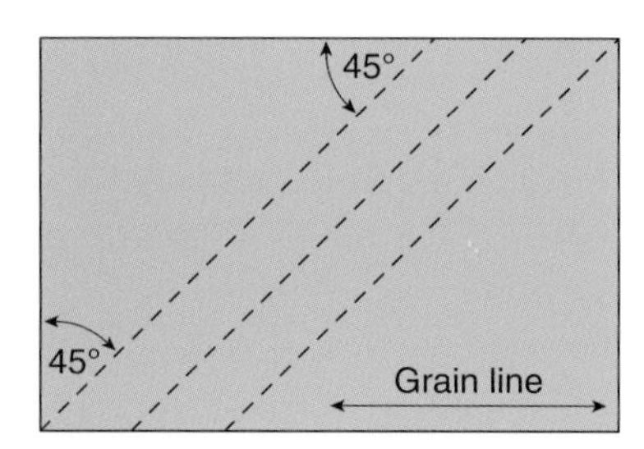

2. Whether you're working with straight- or bias-grain strips, sew the strips together with diagonal seams to eliminate bulk.

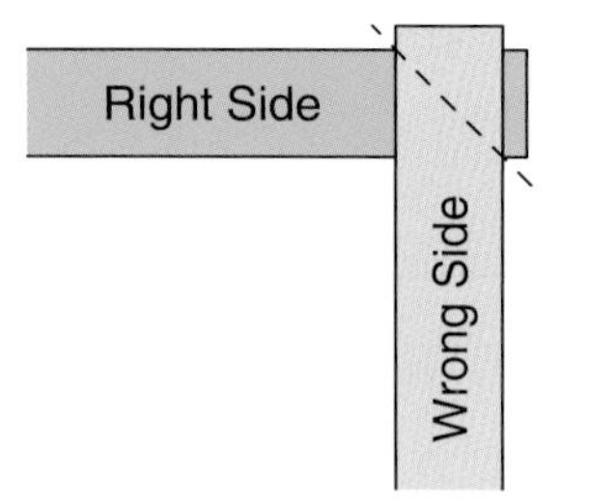

3. Trim each seam to ¼" and press it open. Continue adding strips until you have one long strip that's equal to the length of the filler cord.

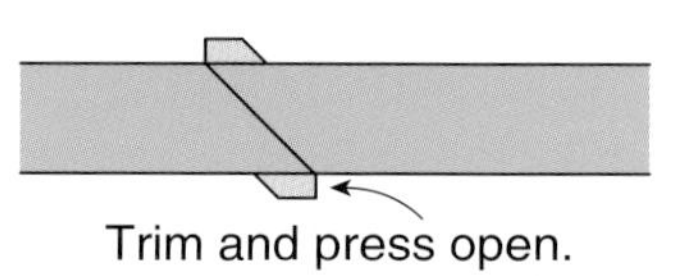

4. Lay the filler cord on the wrong side of the piping strip and wrap the fabric around it, bringing the raw edges together.

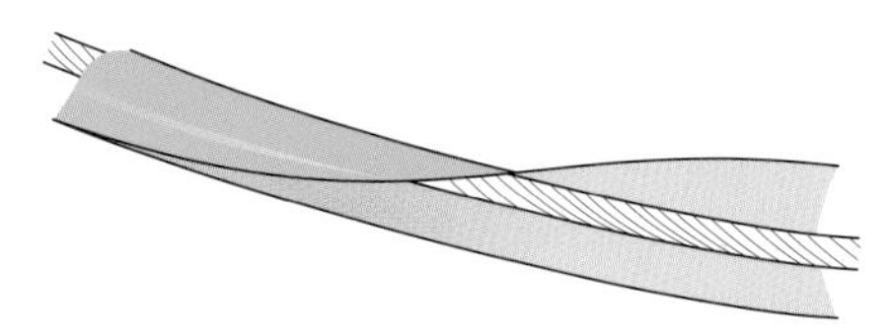

5. Keeping the raw edges aligned, use a cording foot or zipper foot to stitch close to the cord. Be careful not to stretch bias fabric or you'll get puckers in your piping.

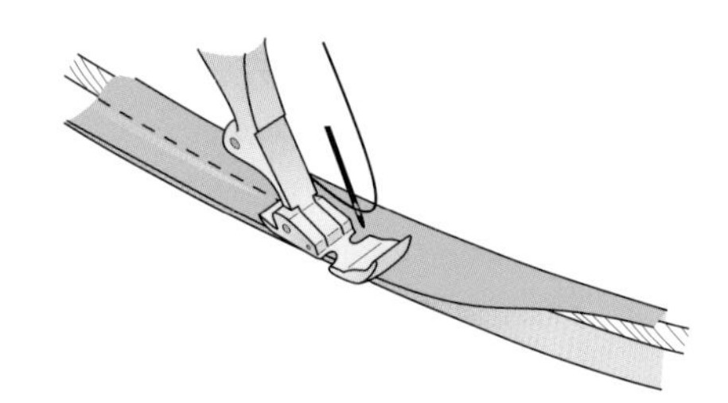

All about Ruffles

Whether lace or fabric, ruffles add impact to the edges of pillows and the tops of stockings. Follow these easy instructions to make ruffles from fabric or flat lace.

Fabric ruffles can be cut on the straight grain or bias. Bias ruffles are curvier. For double-layer ruffles, decide the width and add one seam allowance. Double that number. (If you prefer a single-layer ruffle, decide the width and add one seam allowance and a ½" hem.) The length of a ruffle strip should be 1½ to 2 times the project's perimeter. Cut strips, sew them together, and press the seams as directed in steps 2 and 3, *opposite*. For a pillow, sew the strips together to make a big circle. (Sew the ends of flat lace together in a straight seam.)

Fold the double-layer strip in half. Leave the folded edge unpressed for a soft, rounded edge or press for a sharp edge. (Hem one edge of a single-layer ruffle.) Sew a gathering thread on the seam line (⅓" or ½" from the raw edge) the length of the ruffle or flat lace (through both layers of fabric for double-layer ruffles).

1. Pull up the gathers until the circle of fabric fits around the perimeter of the project. Distribute the gathers evenly,

pushing a little extra into each corner of the pillow and pin—better yet, baste—in place, aligning raw edges. The gathers should align with the seam line of the project.

2. Layer the project front and back, and sew together.

Apply pregathered lace, available in fabric stores, in the same manner as ruffles, except fold the beginning edge under ¼" to ½" so you can slip-stitch it to the ending edge after the project is sewn together.

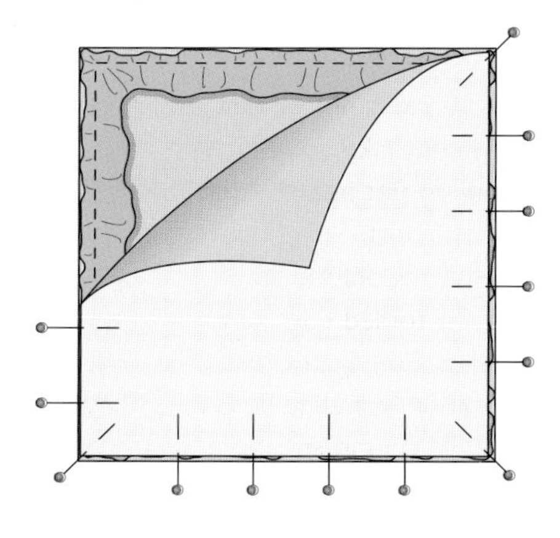

Applying Piping

3. Baste or pin the homemade piping to the outer edge of the right side of the project front, aligning raw edges. (The piping's stitching line should align with the project's seam line.) To fit around

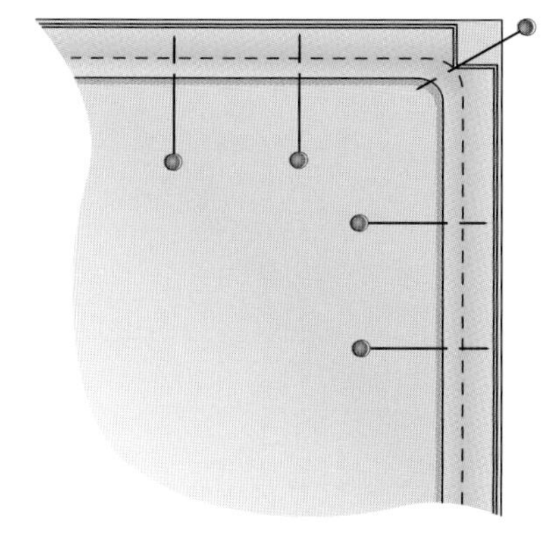

sharp corners, such as those on a square pillow, clip the piping's seam allowance from the raw edge to the stitching.

4. On a pillow front or other project where the ends of piping will join, leave one end of the piping unstitched for the last 3" to 5" (more for thicker piping). Clip away the cord at the end of the stitching. If the end of the fabric isn't already cut at a 45-degree angle, trim it to that angle and press the edge under ¼". Begin basting the unstitched diagonal end to the middle of one side.

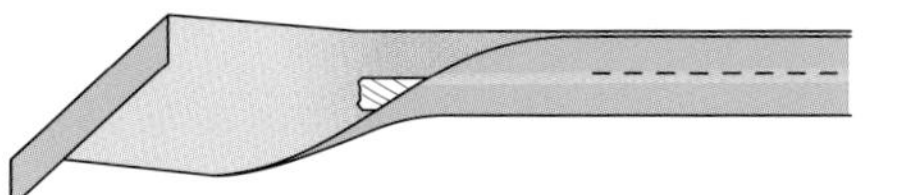

5. After basting or pinning the piping around the pillow, trim the end of the piping so the two ends of the cording butt together.

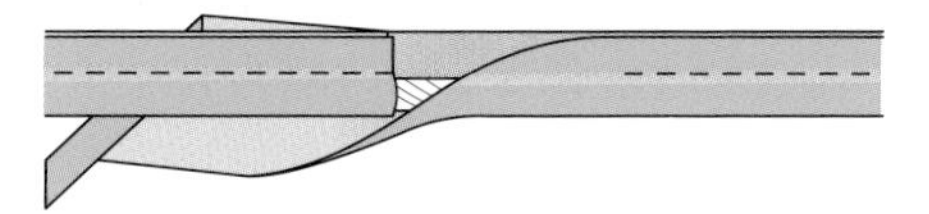

6. Wrap the starting-end fabric around the ending fabric and cord, and baste or pin. Layer the project front and back, and sew together as directed in the project instructions.

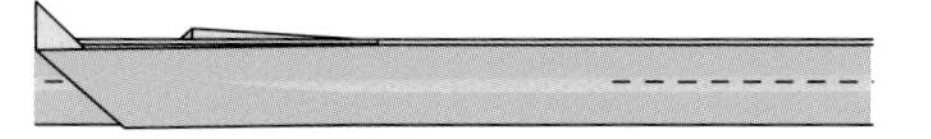

Other Trims

Apply purchased cording, fringe, and other trims with a lip or flange in the same manner as piping, except cross the ends, and baste or pin them so they extend into the seam allowance. Center rickrack on the project's seam line.

Pillows

Stuff It

The back for your pillow depends on whether you stuff the pillow yourself with polyester stuffing, purchase a pillow form, or make a pillow form. To simply fill the pillow with polyester stuffing, plan for a one-piece back. Fabric stores carry premade pillow forms in a variety of standard sizes and shapes. For a pillow that doesn't match a standard size, sew a muslin duplicate of the pillow with a one-piece back and firmly stuff with polyester stuffing. Any pillow with an overlapped or zippered opening should be stuffed with a pillow form.

Back It Up

One-piece back: For this easy pillow back, use the completed front as a pattern for cutting. Stitch the two pieces together along all four sides, but leave a 6" to 8" opening (or larger, if using a pillow form) for turning. Clip the corners diagonally to eliminate excess bulk (see diagram *below*). Turn the pillow right side out; press. Fill the pillow with stuffing or insert a pillow form. Fold the opening's raw edges to the inside along the seam lines. Hand-stitch the folds together.

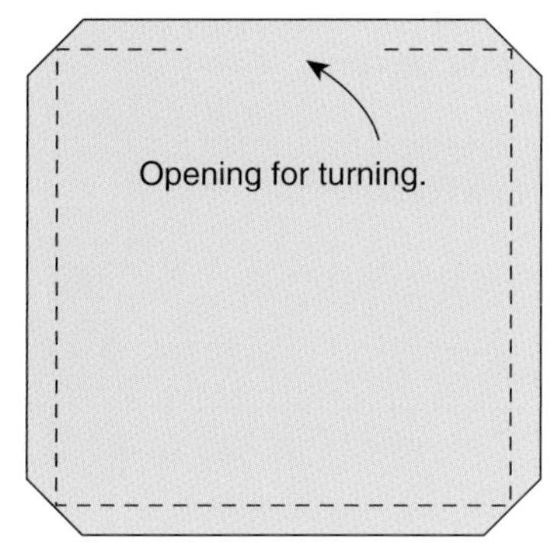

One-piece back

Finish Like a Pro

Overlapped openings: Cut two pieces of fabric, each the same width of the trimmed front and ⅔ to ¾ the length (see cutting diagram *below*). Hem one widthwise edge on each piece. Lay one back piece on the front, right sides together, with the hemmed edge toward the center of the front and the other three edges aligned. Lay the second piece on top of the first so the hemmed edges overlap (see stitching diagram *below*). Stitch around the pillow. Clip the corners diagonally. Turn the pillow right side out through the hemmed edges and insert a pillow form.

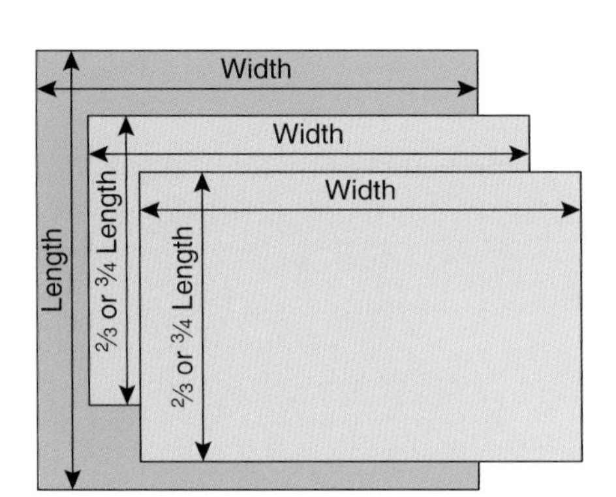

Overlapped opening – Cutting

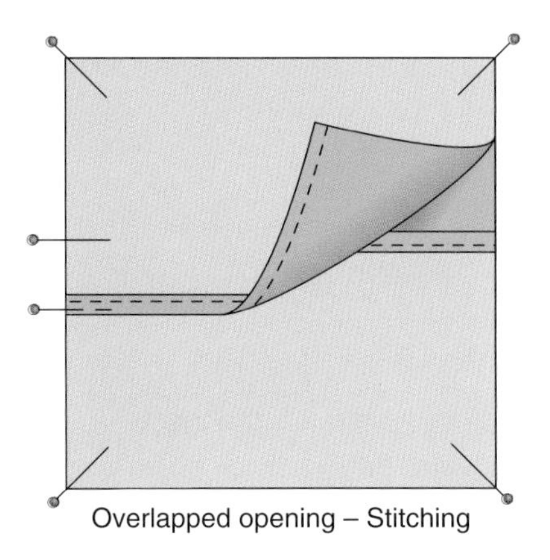
Overlapped opening – Stitching

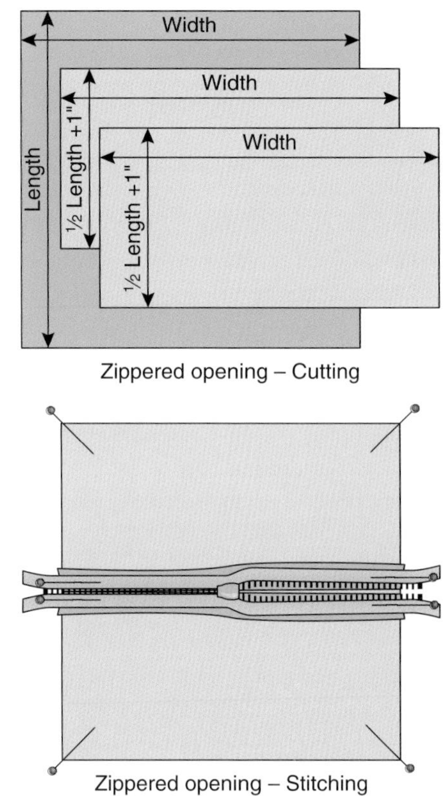

Zippered opening – Cutting

Zippered opening – Stitching

Zippered opening: Purchase a zipper at least 2" longer than the width of the pillow front. Fold the trimmed front in half and measure it. Add 1" along the folded edge. Cut two pieces of fabric that size (see cutting diagram *above*). Apply the zipper between the edges that correspond to the fold on the front. Close the zipper and trim the fabric to match the front; *do not* trim the zipper yet. Pin the front to the back around the edges of the pillow, placing pins as needed (see stitching diagram *above*). Sew around the pillow, back-stitching over the zipper teeth on both sides. Trim the zipper and clip the corners diagonally. Unzip the zipper, turn the pillow right side out, and insert a pillow form.

Stockings

1. If you want to add a sew-in trim to the foot of your stocking, baste it around the edges, Sew the stocking front to the back, leaving the top open. Clip the curves (use scissors to make small cuts from the raw edge to the seam on inward curves). Then turn the stocking right side out and press.
2. If the stocking has a cuff, sew it together as your pattern directs, leaving the top edge unfinished. Slip the cuff onto the stocking, aligning the raw edges, and baste them together. Or baste a trim such as sew-in cord, piping, or a ruffle to the top edge of the stocking with raw edges aligned.
3. Sew together the lining pieces in the same manner as the stocking, except stop halfway up one side and backstitch three or four stitches. Moving along the same edge, start sewing again, beginning with a few backstitches. Clip the curves, but leave the lining wrong side out.
4. Insert the stocking (and cuff or trim, if present) into the lining and align the top edges.
5. Sew all the way around the top, stitching through all layers.
6. Begin pulling the toe of the stocking through the opening in the lining. Continue pulling until the entire stocking and lining are right side out.
7. By hand, slip-stitch to close the opening in the lining.
8. Tuck the lining inside the stocking; press.

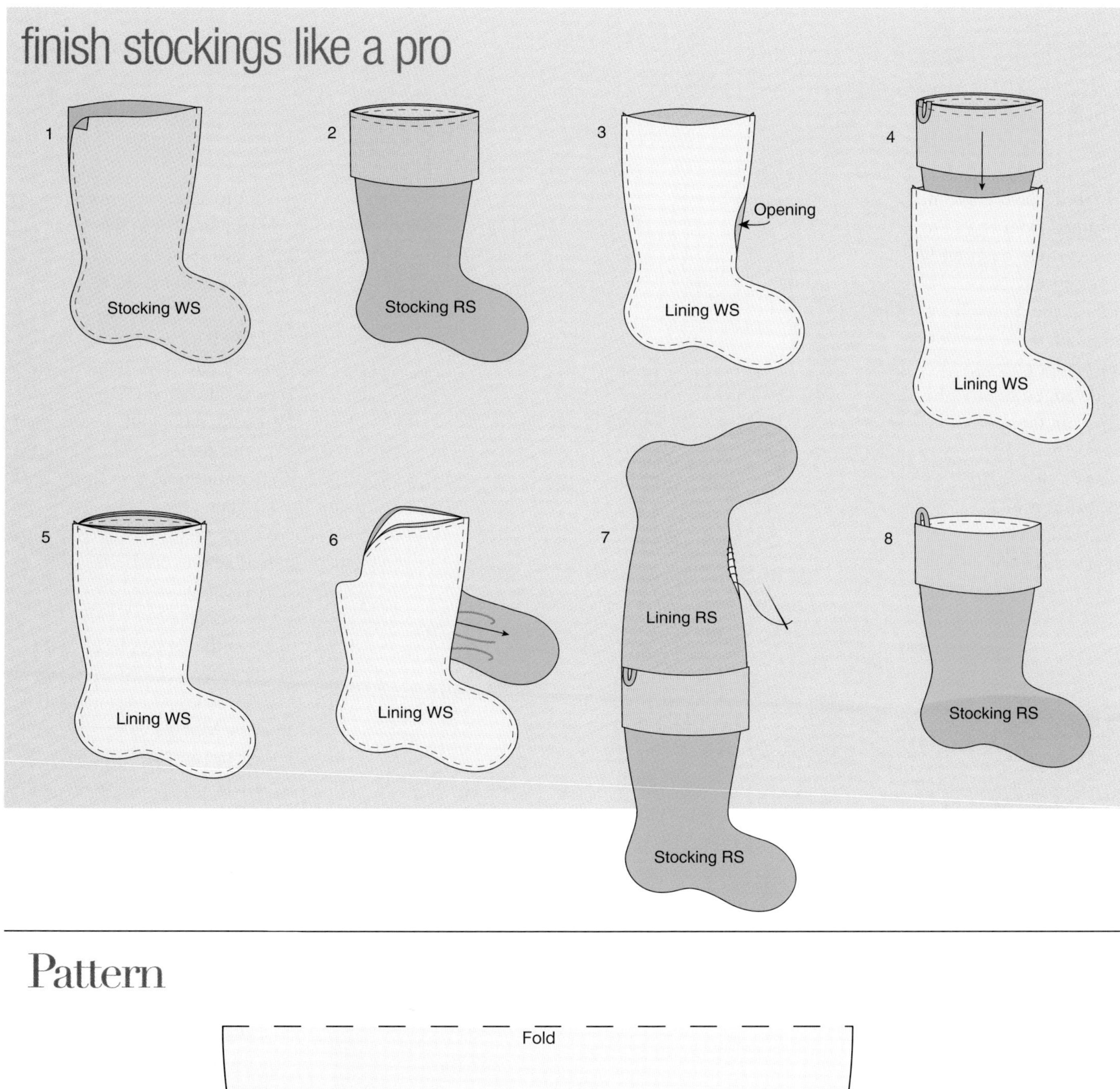

Pattern

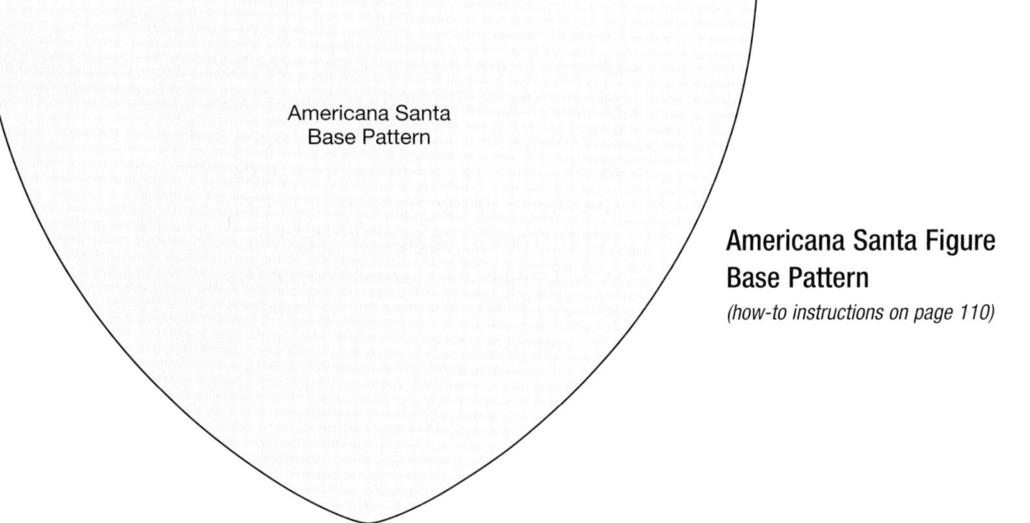

Americana Santa Figure Base Pattern

(how-to instructions on page 110)

Index

T-W

Sources

Many of the materials and items used in this book are available at needlework and crafts stores. For more information, contact the manufacturers or suppliers listed below.

FABRICS
Charles Craft, P.O. Box 1049, Laurinburg, NC 28352; www.charlescraft.com

Wichelt Imports, Inc., N162 State Highway 35, Stoddard, WI 54658; www.wichelt.com

Zweigart, 2 Riverview Dr., Somerset, NJ 08873-1139; www.zweigart.com

THREADS
Anchor, Consumer Services, P.O. Box 12229, Greenville, SC 29612; www.coatsandclark.com

DMC, Port Kearney Bldg. 10, South Kearney, NJ 07032-0650; www.dmc-usa.com

Gentle Art, 4081 Bremo Recess, New Albany, OH 43054; 614/855-8346; fax 614/855-4298; e-mail: gentleart@aol.com

Kreinik Manufacturing Co., Inc.; 800/537-2166 or Daisy Chain, P.O. Box 1258, Parkersburg, VA 26102; www.kreinik.com

BEADS
Mill Hill Beads, Gay Bowles Sales, Inc., P.O. Box 1060, Janesville, WI 53547-1060; 800/447-1332; www.millhill.com

FRAMING
Dot's Gallery and Custom Frame Shop, 4223 Fleur Dr., Des Moines, IA 50321; 515/285-1994

FINISHED ITEMS FOR USE WITH CROSS-STITCH
Sudberry House, 12 Colton Rd., East Lyme, CT 06333; www.sudberry.com

CHAPTER 1—SYMBOLS OF THE SEASON
Nativity, *page 7:* Navy Jobelan fabric—Wichelt Imports, Inc.
Nostalgic Santa Stocking, *page 8:* Raw Dublin linen—Wichelt Imports, Inc.; Zweigart.
Santa, Rag Doll, and Teddy Bear Ornaments, *page 9:* Antique white Aida cloth—Charles Craft; Wichelt Imports, Inc.; Zweigart.
Snow Angel Blessings, *page 10:* Belfast linen—Zweigart.
Snow Angel Blessings Ornament, *page 11:* Ivory Aida cloth—Charles Craft; Wichelt Imports, Inc.; Zweigart.
Tree Place Mat and Star Napkin, *page 12:* Lambswool Jobelan fabric—Wichelt Imports, Inc.
Patchwork Cardinal Tray, *page 13:* Lambswool Jobelan fabric—Wichelt Imports, Inc.; square wood tray (#60131)—Sudberry House.

CHAPTER 2—DECK THE HALLS
Ornament Box tray, *page 26:* Jubilee fabric—Zweigart; wood tray (#65008)—Sudberry House.
Della Robbia Table Runner, Pear Napkin, Holly Napkin Ring, *pages 28–29:* Cameo peach Jobelan fabric—Wichelt Imports, Inc.
Pear Candleholder, *pages 29, 39:* Cameo peach Jobelan fabric—Wichelt Imports, Inc.; Dreamer's Candle Holder by Tracy Porter, available from Walnut Hollow; www.walnuthollow.com; acrylic paint, crackle finish—Delta Technical Coatings, www.deltacrafts.com.
Merry Christmas Sampler, *page 40:* Beige Aida cloth—Wichelt Imports, Inc.
Peace Hurricane Wrap, *page 41:* Raw Glasgow linen—Zweigart; overdyed floss—Needle Necessities, 7211 Garden Grove Blvd., #BC, Garden Grove, CA 92841; www.needlenecessities.com; metallic threads—Kreinik; seed beads—Mill Hill.
Poinsettia Box, *page 32:* Canister Set (#1993)—The Bushel Basket; www.thebushelbasket.com.
Poinsettia Tray, *page 33:* Summer khaki Lugana fabric—Zweigart; rectangular wood tray (#65658)—Sudberry House.
Holly Pillow, *page 34:* Black Aida cloth—Wichelt Imports, Inc.; Zweigart.

CHAPTER 3—SNOWMAN CELEBRATION
Snowman with Toys, *page 54:* Wedgwood Lugana fabric—Zweigart.
Gingham Snowman Pillow, *page 56:* Riviera gingham fabric—Graziano, available from Norden Crafts Ltd., 847/891-0770; www.nordencrafts.com; sampler threads—Gentle Art.
Gingham Snowman Ornament, *page 57:* Jubilee fabric—Zweigart; sampler threads—Gentle Art.
Snowman and Snow Woman Stockings, *page 58:* Navy Aida cloth—Wichelt Imports, Inc.; Zweigart.
Let It Snow!, *page 59:* Beige Aida cloth—Wichelt Imports, Inc.
Snowman in Woods, *page 60:* Silk gauze, Silk Mori—Kreinik.
Snowman in the Woods Pillow, *page 61:* Klostern fabric—Zweigart. Polyester fiberfill—Fairfield Processing Corp.; www.poly-fil.com.

CHAPTER 4—FESTIVE GREETINGS
Christmas Quilt Wall Hanging, *page 73:* Lambswool Jobelan fabric—Wichelt Imports, Inc.
Christmas Quilt Place Mat and Napkin, *page 74:* Country oatmeal place mat—Charles Craft.
Christmas Quilt Ornaments, *pages 74, 81:* Perforated plastic—Darice; www.darice.com. Aida cloth—Charles Craft, Wichelt Imports, Inc., Zweigart.
Keep Christmas in Your Heart, *page 75:* Navy Heatherfield fabric, buttons—Wichelt Imports, Inc.
Noel Ornament, *page 76:* Natural linen—Wichelt Imports, Inc.
No Peeking Ornament, *page 76:* Light espresso linen—R & R Reproductions, 4265 Derby Wharf Dr., Virginia Beach, VA 23456; e-mail: wedye4you@aol.com.
Warmest Wishes, *page 77:* Natural brown linen—Wichelt Imports, Inc.; suede—Tandy Leather Company; www.tandyleather.com.
Christmas in the Country, *page 78:* Belfast linen—Wichelt Imports, Inc.; Zweigart.
Christmas in the Country Ornaments, *page 78:* Perforated plastic—Darice; www.darice.com.
Holiday Stocking, *page 79:* Tula fabric—Wichelt Imports, Inc.; Zweigart.

CHAPTER 5—COME HOME TO CHRISTMAS
Holiday Joy Hardanger, *page 93:* Cream Cashel linen—Zweigart; pearl cotton—DMC.
I Love Christmas, *page 94:* Driftwood Dublin linen—Zweigart; seed beads—Mill Hill.
Favorite Things, *page 95:* Edinburgh linen—Wichelt Imports, Inc.; Zweigart. Metallic threads–Kreinik.
Nordic Stocking Ornaments, *page 96:* Antique white Aida cloth—Charles Craft; Wichelt Imports, Inc.; Zweigart. Dark blue, tartan green Aida cloth—Wichelt Imports, Inc. Victorian red Aida cloth—Zweigart.
Toile Sampler, *page 97:* Pussy willow Aida cloth—Wichelt Imports, Inc.
Believe Angel, *page 98:* Antique white Lugana fabric—Zweigart.
Rag Bag Santa, *page 98:* Raw Belfast linen—Wichelt Imports, Inc., Zweigart.
Americana Santa Stocking, *page 99:* Antique white Aida cloth—Charles Craft; Wichelt Imports. Inc.; Zweigart.
Americana Santa Figure, *page 111:* Antique white Aida cloth—Charles Craft; Wichelt Imports. Inc.; Zweigart.
Deer Gift Tags, *page 107:* Pussy willow Aida cloth—Wichelt Imports, Inc.